SHADES OF REALITY

Short Stories by
Shaykh Fadhlalla Haeri

SHADES OF REALITY

Short Stories by
Shaykh Fadhlalla Haeri

Zahra Publications

Zahra Publications

Published by Zahra Publications
www.shaykhfadhlallahaeri.com
info@shaykhfadhlallahaeri.com
www.zahrapublications.pub

© Shaykh Fadhlalla Haeri, 2024

All rights reserved. Except for brief quotations in critical articles or reviews, no part of this book may be reproduced in any manner without prior written permission from Zahra Publications.

Copying and redistribution of this book is strictly prohibited. Designed and typeset in South Africa by Quintessence Publishing

Set in 11 points on 16 points, Palatino Linotype
Printed and bound by Lightning Source

ISBN (Printed Version) — Paperback: 978-1-7764901-4-1

Table of Contents

INTRODUCTION ---- viii
1 To Take or Not To Take ---- 1
2 East West Ashram ---- 5
3 Lost and Found ---- 9
4 A Diamond in the Rough ---- 13
5 Earthly Love, Heavenly Bliss ---- 17
6 Tabrizi, the Carpet Merchant ---- 21
7 Art of Oblivion ---- 25
8 The Shopping List ---- 31
9 The Banana Farm ---- 35
10 Zoo Lake Celebration ---- 39
11 Isabel in Salzburg ---- 43
12 Supernatural Leader ---- 47
13 Samandari Baba ---- 51
14 Father of the Turks ---- 55
15 The Necklace ---- 61
16 The Failed Sufi ---- 63
17 Meccan Sisters ---- 67

18 The Allure of Sufala --- 71

19 Abdul Jabbar – The Sangoma from Mozambique ------ 75

20 El Millonario -- 79

21 The Jewish Catholic Sufi --------------------------------------- 83

22 Cleopatra's Carpet -- 89

23 Journey to Healing-- 93

24 The Man on the Mountain ---------------------------------- 99

25 The Woman in the Grave ----------------------------------- 103

26 Meshti--- 107

27 The Ramana holiday -- 111

28 The Story of Hayy bin Yaqdhan --------------------------- 115

29 Aziza Begum --- 119

30 Futile Success --- 123

31 Pedro and Son -- 127

32 The Heartless Mufti --- 131

33 Father Fey of Kirkuk -- 135

34 Orlando's Farm--- 139

35 The Palestinians --- 143

36 Tajiki Snake Venom--- 153

37 Walking on Water-- 157

38 The Shaykh of the Buffalo --------------------------------- 161

39 Silent Retreat --- 165

40 The Wali of the Atlas Mountains -------------------------- 169

41 Distorted Similarity -- 173

42 Failed Departure	177
43 Laylah al Ahmad	183
44 Sadiq, the Martyr	187
45 Liberating Education	191
46 Uniformed Brutality	195
47 The Empty Cradle	199
48 The Oldest Bridge in Baghdad	203
49 Doors, not Window	207
50 Sakina House	213
51 Sai Baba	217
52 The Prisoner	221
53 Warren Shaw	225
54 The Heirloom	229
55 Barberton Gold	233
56 Awakened by Death	237
57 Qalandari Baba	241
58 Omar, the Silent	245
59 Murder at Bari Imam	249
60 Indignant Indigenous	253
61 The Green Man	257
62 The Medical Rep	265
63 Maha, the Bahá'í Iranian	269
64 Arjun's Burden	273
65 The Saint of Bombay	275

INTRODUCTION

Human life is a complex puzzle. Two living cells unite and grow into billions of cells and produce a unique being. Everyone is different, but also similar in seeking contentment, happiness, ease, security, and hope for a better future. However, we experience suffering, regret and a whole range of negative emotions. Thus we hope that tomorrow will be better. More importantly, we hope that our experience after death will be more enjoyable and blissful than earthly life.

It is obvious to an intelligent thinker that we live in a zone of consciousness that is hazy at best. You think something is certain, but the next moment it may be less certain. In fact, everything regarding our senses or understanding is imprecise. Time, for example, is experienced as emerging from stillness and timelessness. Time and space delineates human consciousness on earth, which is conditioned by genetic, historical, environmental, cultural and parental influences.

Even though everything is changeable at any moment, we yearn for constancy, certainty and security. Death is the gateway to another state of consciousness without human interference. Until then, we live in the zone of conditioned consciousness where time and space limits us. While we are here we can figure out the puzzle of time and its emergence from an energy source that is often referred to as God or the Divine – which is timeless and eternal.

Consciousness and intelligence have been rising since the beginning of creation and will eventually return to the original Source where the limits of space and time don't exist. For now, we are restricted within space and time and all of our problems come from this confined state. Souls, however, are not subject to this state of limitations. It is on a short earthly journey before it returns to its immaculate state when we die, when the veil of the body and emotions is finally lifted. In the meantime, we will only catch glimpses or flashes of the true eternal Reality.

In these stories I would like to show the many different ways that people strive towards a better life that is more secure and enjoyable. Sometimes our lives may be in a downward spiral and it might feel as if everything is disintegrating on a path of entropy. Our journey on earth is a short period of being exposed to interaction with the outer world, a period of awareness and self-reflection, which often follows a path that touches both hope and despair. I hope these snippets of life will enable the reader to rise in awareness to the inner spirit, which is eternal and divine.

1
To Take or Not To Take

High up in the Himalayas, where it snows most of the year, there was a village where people lived a simple and harmonious life. Colourful Buddhist prayer flags were fluttering everywhere.

The local rulers used to send emissaries to different parts of the land to find acknowledged teachers and then invited them to their village. Every few decades they had a new teacher who would revive the old traditions, thus avoiding the pitfall of a ceremonial ritualistic way of life.

A time came when they heard that an old Buddhist master had arrived in the area and was staying at a nearby village on the bank of the river. The villagers were eager to learn more about his meditative practices so a few representatives were sent to invite the great teacher to visit their village.

After spending a week with the people the Master asked the villagers to select a dozen men and women with whom he would spend some time to teach them everything he knew, after which they should teach others.

He taught them that human life is based on two zones of consciousness and awareness. One is practical and causal, based on opposites: good and bad, beginnings and ends, birth and death. This zone is given to us so that we can transact with other people and life around us. The other is not bound by time and space and that is where our eternal soul resides. To experience this higher consciousness we need to transcend all dualities by love, affection and silence until a wave of grace blows us into the perfect light of eternal Reality.

We are part of nature and need to respect the natural flow. All the millions of creatures and plants have to stay in equilibrium. Respect for all life is paramount, from the smallest ant to the gigantic blue whale.

After a few months the Master announced that it was time to test and apply everything that they had learnt. He asked them to prepare for a journey on horseback, taking as little food or belongings as possible. They would be sustained by Mother Nature.

It was a particularly hot summer, therefore they chose to travel by night. During the day they meditated, foraged for food to share and filled up their water sacks. On the second night they crossed a valley next to a river. They noticed sparks flying from the hooves of the horses. Some of them stopped, dismounted and collected some of the pebbles. The Master saw this and said, "Whoever picks up these pebbles will regret it tomorrow morning, and those who don't, will regret it too."

Just before sunrise they decided to rest and the pebble collectors were astonished to find that they had in their possession valuable semi-precious stones. They immediately regretted not picking up more. Those who did not pick up any pebbles regretted it all the more.

The Master gathered them round and told them, "This is how life is. When you acquire or control an aspect of it, physical, emotional or mental, you feel good, as if you have accomplished something. But soon regret sets in and you realize your new attachment was a mistake. You think you have made a mistake. For the new car you need insurance, for the big house you need staff to help maintain it, and as for the partner, as you get to know each other, you doubt whether this was the best match for you. Last night you have moved across the valley of life. If you take from it, you regret it; if you don't take from it, you also regret it.

"But this is what life is. You can't escape it, you have to accept it. You have to give and you have to take, or not give and not take. To cope with life you have to follow the middle path between the extremes of self-denial and self-indulgence, always aware that there is no reliable and constant self. It is a mere shadow of the ever-living soul. You are just a miraculous combination of chemical elements that make up your physical body. We are between physics and metaphysics, heavenly and earthly, this life and the hereafter. Our challenge is to be on earth while at the same time recalibrating with higher consciousness.

"In life you cannot choose if you want to be involved in giving and taking; occasionally you give, occasionally you take. As you grow in knowledge about the divine nature of life, you will recognise your past illusions of independence. While you go about your earthly life you must also be at one with the inner divine presence."

2
East West Ashram

Andrew was in his third year at the East West Ashram on the outskirts of Bombay, where he had taken the oath of celibacy. After his acrimonious divorce in London, he had lost all interest in his career as a stockbroker. His wife took over the house, the dog and the holiday villa in the south of France. She had even accused him of trying to kill her in a dramatic skiing accident. After a few months of taking ineffective psychiatric medication, he ended up at the sprawling ashram.

Destiny is often a great mystery and no one can be certain of its outcome.

As a child, Andrew believed that he could talk to animals and even fly with birds. In his childhood he had been influenced by various ideas of the paranormal and supernatural. He liked to read about the saints of Christian mysticism and Saint Francis of Assisi had been his favourite. Before he left Britain he attended several meditation courses and even imagined himself levitating and being able to do distance viewing.

Initially his main interest at the ashram was to find out what the Brahmins and Yogis were aiming to achieve. He was pleasantly surprised to find that Hindu meditation and chanting was very helpful in his practice of transcendence.

He loved his master, Guruji, unconditionally and trusted him completely. Guruji had spent more than twenty years high up in the Himalayas, almost naked. He almost never ate and his body had changed dramatically; most notably he had lost all the hair on his head and body. People from medical schools had studied him and even performed minor experiments. One such experiment involved piercing his muscles with needles. They were astounded to find that he didn't react to the pain at all. Incredibly, no blood appeared from these wounds.

One day there was an incident that made Andrew question his trust in the Guru. A poor, old peasant from Bihar arrived at the ashram with the hope to understand what happens after death before he died himself. He had spoken to a few swamis and gurus about it, but their answers had not satisfied him. Apparently the old man had sold most of his belongings before he made his way to the ashram in Bombay.

When he first arrived, he was allowed to stay one week as a guest, but he had to leave immediately after that. He attended daily discourses stretching from dawn to midday with a breakfast in between. Andrew wrote about these discourses in his journal. He considered it the most profound teaching he had received in his life, especially learning about the dual nature of humanity. If you want to know the truth of who you are, you must leave all illusion and anything that had happened to you. Through silence and meditation you may catch a glimpse of higher consciousness, pure and divine.

A few days later during the dawn discourse, Andrew found the old man prostrated before the Guru, asking in a humble whisper if he could stay longer. However the gentle and compassionate Swami was unwavering and insisted that the peasant leave that day as had been agreed. This lack of kindness by his "perfect" Guru puzzled Andrew. He asked himself, where is the justice, where is the unconditional generosity? The poor man had reached a point in his life where he had forsaken everything, except the desire to know, to be sure about the state after death and now he had to leave without a clear answer.

After breakfast, he saw the peasant with his stick and bundle of belongings, walking the mile long stretch towards the gate. He had been curious to know if the man was content to leave, so he caught up with him and started talking to him about his visit. Andrew asked him directly if he was happy with his stay and if he had received what he came for. The old man answered with a cheerful face, "Yes, I am very happy, I got it all!"

At first Andrew was perplexed by the man's response, but a few days later he understood that his Guru had acted from a position of higher intelligence, where he knew that if you give people more time and more opportunity, the issue of doubt and procrastination can stretch itself out endlessly. The Guru knew that if he didn't put an end to the man's quest for answers, he would remain in constant doubt.

Truth is ever-present in the moment.

3
Lost and Found

The warm rays of the morning sun brought Nico back to life. He was lying on the sand, and with the tide coming in again, small waves were washing over him with the eternal rhythm of the ocean.

For three days he had been adrift in the sea between the islands of Mallorca and Minorca. His small inflatable dingy must have had a slow puncture and sank an hour or so after he left early in the morning. The few hours of solitude on the water he had planned turned into a whole day drifting aimlessly at sea. He was sure he would be rescued before dusk, but as the sun set he knew he would probably have to spend the night at sea. That first night he did not lose hope. He was grateful for the warm weather and floating on his back he marveled at the wide expanse of stars. But when a second day passed with no rescue fear and hopelessness crept in. By the third night he was so weak, confused, and close to hallucinating, that he just gave up and waited for death to free him from his misery.

He lifted his head from the sand and saw a few kids splashing about on the beach in the distance. He lost consciousness again for a while and woke up hearing a woman's voice asking if he was okay. The glare of the sun was excruciating, and he thought he might be hallucinating. "My name is Maria," the voice came again. "Do you need help?" In a hoarse voice Nico managed to reply, "Water, please. Water."

A while later, safely on Maria's family boat, he told her the saga of his last three days and nights, how he constantly drifted in and out of consciousness. Strangely, he was tremendously grateful for having experienced life and death so frequently. He let out a sigh and said that it felt as if a veil was lifted, as if he was now able to see the beauty and perfection in every situation. He felt as if he was now living beyond the norms of everyday life. Maria sat next to him, hanging onto every word, surprised and thrilled to hear his touching story.

Nico sat back, closed his eyes and a big smile appeared on his cracked and sunburnt face. He could hear the children's laughter above the sound of the sea, the waters that almost killed him, but had also saved him in a way that he could never have dreamt of. "This is the most perfect day," he said, "and I am the most joyful man alive. Sitting here, I realize that all my life's fears, concerns, hopes and desires are to no avail. And I owe all of this to being completely lost at sea, simply drifting from one moment to another with no idea about past or future. Life's pure raw power is always there, but we restrict it because of our limited consciousness. Why? Why do we do that? Just to preserve and prolong our biological life! I am going to break loose from that cocoon of constant care about survival."

Maria looked to the horizon and swallowed the lump in her throat. She thought about her own life and her daily meditations, which she was convinced had enlightened her little by little over the years. But she realized that only on a few occasions had she ever touched upon such a state of simple being-ness that Nico was describing.

As Nico was preparing to leave, a series of expressions of gratitude volleyed between the two of them.

"Thank you so much for saving me from the tide today."

"I should be thanking you for coming into my life today. Your story has awakened a fresh curiosity in me."

"No, really, I owe my life to you. I would have been drawn right back into the sea if it wasn't for you."

"Well, it seems like you are not the only one who was lost, and I had to rescue you so that you could save me. Thank you, Nico, for sharing the newfound peace in your heart."

Nico left the boat feeling light and free from fears or the desire for freedom, much more eager to face any aspect of the distractions and the distortions of everyday life.

Waving goodbye, Maria shed a few tears. She hoped that perhaps one day she would get 'there' too, to a place within herself where time and space ceased to exist. Where she could lose herself and just feel the connection with the source of life. Nico's parting words still rang in her ears. "Everyone is so entangled with their own illusions and so they can never reach a desirable conclusion."

Once the soul is ready to give up its illusion of separateness, then we realize that there is only immortality.

4
A Diamond in the Rough

Lost in thought, with a small plate of food forgotten in my one hand, I heard a loud gasp followed by a sob. I looked around the room, only to find that it was Saleemah, my sister, who was sitting right next to me on a couch. Her body was shaking trying to hold back the tears. We had just attended our Aunty Fatima's funeral and my sister seemed to be hit hard by her passing. This perplexed me because our aunt had had a long life and did not die unexpectedly.

I put an arm around her shoulders and pulled her closer. Wiping the tears from her eyes, she whispered somberly in my ear, "I don't want to die like she did, all by herself in her apartment. She must have passed away during the night … hours before Dr Habib came for his morning visit. She died alone; it is just … just … heartbreaking."

Just before Aunty Fatima's death, her cousin Ahmed, who loved her deeply, had spent some time with her. His aunt was already very frail, the pain from rheumatism showing in every movement, and he was worried that she would die without peace of mind. "What is it that you hold dear in this life, Aunty?" Ahmed asked her. After some thought she answered, "The Qur'an – that is what I hold dearest. It has always been my companion and compass in life. But the inhuman behavior of pretentious Muslims upsets me intensely."

Ahmed knew that she still held a grudge against her late husband, Dr Ameen, who had brought her much shame and grief. He had been an overly ambitious businessman and political predator, always onto the next big money making scheme, which landed him in serious trouble several times. After being sued for medical malpractice early on in his career for overprescribing questionable beta blockers, he was also accused of lacking a medical qualification. Dr Ameen claimed that the records containing his name disappeared in the fire that had destroyed much of the medical school in Mauritius in 1961, where he had studied medicine. Even though many people didn't believe him, he was reinstated, but soon thereafter he stopped practicing medicine and began a new career importing and distributing generic drugs from India and China. After three years he had to close the unprofitable business and started a new career once again, this time in 'mining'.

The thing about her husband that pained Aunty Fatima the most though was his religious pretensions. For many years he had been a prominent committee member of two of the main mosques in town. Most people looked up to him and regarded him as an important and respectable member of the community. Once, when a certain mullah objected to the marriage Ameen had arranged for his niece, Ameen was so furious that he got the preacher dismissed. Yet, Ameen maintained his good standing in the community by making frequent contributions to charities.

For someone like Aunty Fatima, who loved and trusted the Qur'an, her husband's behavior and that of many others like him was especially hurtful. Ahmed could see that the memories of her turbulent life distressed her. She looked at him and almost whispering, she said, "I know deep in my heart that if the Muslims just returned to the Book and really applied it in their lives, they will be directed toward the ultimate purpose of life."

"I cannot agree with you more, Aunty Fatima," Ahmed replied. "I have an idea. Why don't you set up a trust to create a new type of madrasah that will teach the inner meanings of the Qur'an?" Her eyes lit up and as quickly as she could manage, she got up and disappeared into her bedroom. She reappeared minutes later and in a trembling hand, she held a huge rough diamond. She handed it to Ahmed. He just stared at it, hardly believing his own eyes. The diamond was surely more than 400 carats and even in that rough state, it was probably worth a few million dollars. Wide-eyed he asked, "Where did you get this?"

"Ameen left it to me in his will. But to tell you the truth, I was so disillusioned by him that I just locked it away in the safe and forgot about it. I never even had it valued. Please take it, sell it and build that college."

That night Aunty Fatima had a dream of the Prophet. He came to her and put his cloak around her, thanking her for continuing his work. She tried to look up to him, but somehow, the light around his head prevented her from catching his eye. Still, it was a delightful dream that stayed with her.

When she passed away a week later, the diamond had already been sold with the money safely in a trust and a teacher from Turkey already on his way.

Another muffled sob from my sister brought me back to the present. I put down the plate of food, still untouched, and put both my arms around her and wondered what I could say to cheer her up. "Oh, Saleemah, I know it is hard to accept, but in the end we all actually die alone. It is by its very nature a solitary experience. But think of what Aunty Fatima has left behind – a diamond in the rough that will one day be a beacon of light."

5
Earthly Love, Heavenly Bliss

When we are in pain, time expands; when we experience joy, time shrinks.

In the historic town of Alcúdia on the Spanish island Mallorca, Carlos and Sophia sat on a bench at the bus terminal in sad anticipation of yet another separation. Sophia's head rested on Carlos' shoulder, her face showing signs of recent tears. The short school break was over, meaning Sophia had to go back to the capital, Palma, where she was headmistress of a school for handicapped children. Carlos, a professional painter in the contemporary semi-abstract style, taught art at the local school.

They had met a year ago on the beach while attending a talk by an environmentalist on the endangered local tortoise. Climate change and the booming tourism industry were blamed as the main contributors for the dwindling number of tortoises on the island. Carlos was immediately enamored with Sophia and while the future of the hapless creature was discussed, he drew a picture of a tortoise in a small sketchbook that he always carried with him. In one of the scutes of the shell, he added a tiny portrait of her. When the talk was over, he approached her and offered the sketch to her.

The time of Sophia's departure arrived and as they approached the bus, she started crying again. Carlos held her very close and whispered in her ear, "It is unbearable to be apart from you. This world is too awful to face alone. Being apart feels like a small death, it's just agony. When you go away I am a complete wreck of a being, and it takes a few days before I can pretend to be well again."

That night Carlos fell asleep lulled by the sound of the calm sea. He had left the windows open to let the cool breeze in and to catch glimpses of the water in the moonlight. He had a wonderful dream of Sophia talking to him while cleaning a freshly caught fish. When he woke up and realized that Sophia was not there, he was miserable and even wished he had died in the hypnotic drift of his dream.

Then a wave of anger came over him, and the inevitable question was hurled into the night – why is the real world so cruel? He felt wounded and powerless against the unfairness of life and he started pacing angrily around the room. Uttering a frustrated scream, he hit the wall with his fist. The shock of the pain made him gasp for breath and in that moment, he knew he was going to have to ride the wave of another panic attack. He sat down beside the bed, hugging himself and doing the breathing exercise he was taught to help him calm down. In for a count of four, hold for a count a seven, slowly out, count to eight. Repeat.

When he calmed down a little bit, he felt the need to talk to someone. Someone that might have an answer for him. He got up and walked to his huge, messy desk. Under a pile of papers he found the phone and dialed his father's number.

Carlos's father listened patiently to his son's lament and then answered in his soothing baritone voice. "My dear son, you might not believe it, but I remember how it felt to be young and passionate and angry at the world. It took me years to realize how self-centered my grievances were. I must warn you that my answer might frustrate you even more. My answer is this: the world's cruelty is God's way of ensuring that we don't fall in love with earthly life and that we don't learn to trust it to bring us joy. You know that we will all have to die one day, and if life on earth is only moonshine and roses, how will you be able to accept that? The experience of love and companionship just makes this earthly transition more bearable. But when your time comes to leave your body, and you are ready, that is your real liberation. A wise person knows that the bad experiences of being alive on earth are the steppingstones to being ready for the next phase, the hereafter."

Carlos sat staring at the art work of his students that he still needed to grade. His hand was still on the phone's handset, now resting again in its cradle. The curtains were blowing in the breeze. He looked up and became aware of the sound of the sea again. His father's words had struck a chord within, and he wondered about the gap between what you know is wise and what touches and wrenches your heart. He smiled gently to himself, and said out loud, "Well, I forgot that there are two of me, head and heart. I had better start working on reconciling the two instead of refereeing fights between them."

6
Tabrizi, the Carpet Merchant

"Absolutely exquisite!" my friend, Daniel, exclaims. I am showing him the framed handwoven silk Persian carpet hanging on the wall.

"It was a gift from Tabrizi, the legendary carpet merchant. Incidentally, Tabriz is also a city in the northwest of Iran famous for producing exquisite Persian rugs," I say.

The magnificent handiwork on display boggles the mind. There are about 2000 knots per square inch, but to the untrained eye the texture just looks soft and downy.

Daniel is mesmerized by the carpet and is standing with his nose mere inches away from the carpet on the wall. "It is an interesting combination of colours, though. Very unusual. Not at all what I had expected."

The border is done in cobalt blue and scarlet red, but these colours are not repeated in the main pattern. There, on an off-white background, you see soft brown and pink hues shaping the Farsi letters.

"Yes, this carpet is very old and not done in the later fashionable patterns and colours. I have scrutinized this carpet many times to see if it has an imperfection, but as yet I haven't found any," I say.

Daniel looks perplexed. "Why would there be an imperfection?" he asks.

"It is said that with these handwoven carpets the weavers would always bring in a tiny imperfection as a sign of their humility, for only God is perfect. These imperfections became like a signature for the different master weavers. You can recognize a carpet's origin if you could find the flaw," I explain. "You know, for thousands of years in the old Eastern civilizations, carpets were one of the main assets people had. No respectable home was without a few rugs. And many of them were handed down for several generations. My mother had a beautiful rug, which came from her mother's dowry, which in turn came from my great grandmother's dowry. Carpet weaving provided an income for thousands of villagers."

I can see that Daniel is not too taken with my little snippet of history. As soon as I have finished my sentence, he interjects, "Where is this Tabrizi now? I would love to buy a Persian carpet from him!"

His face falls when I start to chuckle. "I'm so sorry, Daniel, but you are a few decades too late. When I met Tabrizi many years ago he was already in his eighties and furthermore, the art of handwoven carpets had more or less disappeared with his generation."

"But what happened?" a very disappointed Daniel asked.

"Come, let's go and make some coffee, then I will tell you."

With the smell of freshly brewed coffee in our noses, we move to the veranda, and I continue down memory lane.

"Okay, let me start by telling you about the carpet weaving industry. Many years ago, you see, the peasants kept different animals, like, goat, sheep and camels and the villagers became skilled at spinning wool from these creatures and then weaving carpets from it. They dyed the wool with colourants derived from plants growing in their area. Their local leaders started supporting them with materials and dyes and acted as the distributors of these works of art. In many of the older cities in Turkey, Iran, India and Pakistan there would always be a family that was known to link the village weavers to the top end markets. Tabrizi was one of these people. He came from a family that had always dealt with the peasants and helped the weavers obtain whatever they needed to make these superb carpets, whether it was looms, dyes, threads, wool or other raw materials. As you know, carpet weaving became a prestige national industry. And at the peak of Tabrizi's time as a merchant there were approximately half a million weavers in Iran. His family's business grew exponentially, and they had warehouses and stores in Europe, the USA and South America."

With a glimmer of hope in his voice Daniel asks, "Do his shops still exist?"

"No, no," I answer, "after the Iran-Iraq war in the 1980s, Tabrizi had lost interest in the business and started selling all the shops that he had owned. I think he had realized that the carpet weaving industry was changing rapidly. The younger people in these affluent families also saw this and pursued other avenues of wealth. Machine weaving took over and Chinese replicas started to dominate the market.

"What Tabrizi wanted anyway was to take care of Muslim refugees, single parent households and orphans. The wealth that he had created selling Persian carpets made that possible. He established centres for these destitute people as far as Central Asia and remote parts of Turkey. That was what he enjoyed, to travel to these places, stay for a week or two and just spend time with the little ones."

"That is so admirable," Daniel says, and we sit in silence for a while. But it isn't long before he ponders whether some of these handwoven carpets might still be for sale somewhere in the world.

"I doubt that, I think they are all in private collections by now," I say. "Tabrizi himself owned a quite a big Isfahan carpet woven in precious silk by Qajari princesses."

"I'm sorry, did I hear you correctly? Did you say a princess had woven the carpet?" Daniel interrupts in disbelief.

"Yes, yes," I continue, "for centuries the Iranian royal families followed the tradition of teaching princesses how to weave silk carpets, presumably to keep them out of mischief. These carpets would end up as heirlooms and different royal families would also compete to buy them. Often you will find carpet dealers presenting a carpet as being woven by a princess to increase the price and of course nobody will know what the truth is."

"Fascinating," Daniel says. "I wonder how many stories that we accept as historical truth are actually fanciful fabrications."

7
Art of Oblivion

The picture was one of desolation. The burnt willow tree, surrounded by mounds of ashes, stood in its stark magnificence. In the aftermath of the dreadful fire, a single bird perched on the charred branches was the only sign of life. Countless shards of the shimmering, glazed porcelain Neil had been famous for, lay scattered on the ground.

Jack received a phone call from Neil's neighbour, informing him about his brother's demise. An electrical fault had caused an explosion and the subsequent destruction of the workshop, studio and house. As was his custom, Neil had been alone, working in the dead of night to produce the ultimate masterpiece. Like Sisyphus, pushing the stone up the hill just to see it roll down again. Then starting all over again.

Walking around in the debris Jack saw one item had escaped the fire – Belinda's swing. When June, Neil's ex-wife, finally got tired of living with an eccentric genius who rarely spoke to her, she left him and took everything, except their daughter's old swing. Belinda was in her thirties now, married with children, but her childhood swing still remained moving eerily in the breeze.

Neil's passion was for his creations, not other humans, but if he did love anybody it was that little blonde girl with her pigtails, freckles and friendly smile. Whenever Jack visited his niece, she would run into his arms, crying, "Uncle Jack, Uncle Jack, have you bought any sweets for me?" There were no shops for many miles, so Belinda looked to infrequent visitors for her candy fix.

Even as a child Neil was always making something, from scribbling with his crayons on his mother's sofas, yellow sunflowers emerging from the pristine white upholstery, to mixing water with the red earth that surrounded their house to messily mould his first attempts at clay pots, which were literally sun baked.

Art school was inevitable. There was a stoneware period before he discovered his lifelong passion for porcelain vases, tea pots, miniature tea cups, saki cups and sushi plates. He went to Japan to learn his craft. In Kyoto, under the tutelage of a master, the world of shibui, or understated elegance, was revealed to him. Neil was hooked, and slowly but surely mastered the art of the translucent, luminous glaze, the ceramist's most taxing medium. Working with glaze required such attention to detail that Neil easily lost himself completely in the process and became oblivious to all around him, just diving into infinite nothingness. Oblivion came easy to Neil as he always ignored other people's needs or expectations.

Sensei Hitoshi, his Japanese teacher, was like a Zen master in the reverential manner in which he approached his art. His studio was located amidst the temples of Kyoto and no monk worshipped more devotedly than he did at his production altar. Neil was literally like clay in the Sensei's hands, allowing himself to be modelled in the same way as the pots. For the first time in his life he took instruction seriously. Sensei Hitoshi showed him how the creative force comes from the unseen, and no human potter can ever be anything more than a partial channel bringing form from the Formless. There is no predictability about the outcome. Masterpieces will come unannounced, as will the more common failures, nor can a beautiful piece ever be exactly reproduced. The good, the bad and the ugly are all unique one-offs. The good potter must be in a state of humility waiting with hope and prayers for his result.

"The creative exercise," Sensei Hitoshi used to say, "is an act of love. Look at this sushi platter and the variegated hue of colours that have mingled together. To love is to melt in the Beloved's embrace, so too different colours merge together in the potter's furnace, losing differentiation as their boundaries dissolve, all resting upon the celestial bed of earthly clay."

One day in Kyoto Neil noticed the Sensei gently reprimanding his gardener for sweeping away the leaves in front of the studio. "Put the leaves back the way you found them," the Master ordered. It was this attention to the natural order of things that deeply impacted Neil.

His training over, Neil returned to South Africa. He found an outlet in an upmarket Johannesburg art gallery, whose mark-up on his pieces was at least five times what he charged them. Not that Neil minded, as long as he could create he was happy. Every now and then some magazine referred to the up-and-coming potter.

Once a year he would visit Sensei Hitoshi in Kyoto to learn new techniques of glazing and for some soul nourishment to refine his access to inner silence. On one of those visits the Sensei's parting words to him were, "Do not ever think ours is a romantic art, it requires constant dedication and focus. It is joyous, but not romantic!"

Neil eventually bought some land in a remote rural area in the Eastern Cape and set up his workshop there. As always he immersed himself in his work, but it was a struggle to survive as an independent artist, because in the preceding years Neil had fallen from his pedestal. He was forced to make ornamental garden pots to supplement his income. He also had to spend long hours on the road, finding outlets for his work. He needed large quantities of wood for his kilns, as well as a large number of shelves to protect the pieces from blown ash. He became moody and depressed.

Then the rains came and the fire boxes started to disintegrate, and the roof of his shack collapsed. When the weather finally improved, he was able to salvage something from the original building, bemoaning all the time the opportunities for working that he had lost. Neil was somewhat of a pyro-technician, loving to experiment, firing his pieces at the highest possible temperatures, believing it was this level of heat that gave the optimum result.

At this time of transition and difficulty, June entered his life. She ran a shop in George selling decorative items for the home and Neil became one of her suppliers. June had a great desire to be the force behind some artistic genius and soon they were a couple. Not too long after, Belinda came along.

Neil continued his lifelong habit of working at night. He was literally out of the house, day and night. As his work increased, he paid less and less attention to June. The true potter is wedded to his art and

Neil required a more self-effacing and understanding partner. One day, June could bear the loneliness no longer. She packed up her possessions, took Belinda, and left to resume her life in George.

Neil missed his family in some ways, but was equally pleased to have been left alone to pursue his passionate love of oblivion. His workshop grew in size, and soon the expensive galleries in Gauteng and the Cape once again displayed his pieces. He no longer had to make garden pots, and best of all, was able to live a life of total dedication to his art.

When Jack wasn't infuriated by his brother's total disregard for everything except his work, he rather admired his capacity for a fast track to oblivion. For Neil, the alcohol or drugs of lesser mortals held no sway; his demon was the pursuit of that perfect piece of art. Maybe, just before his explosive exit, Neil held in his hand the vase with the perfect honey coloured glaze – his ultimate goal; and knew there was nothing more for him to achieve in this realm of existence.

"Neil was more fortunate than most of us in this robotic age," Jack thought. "He lived a blissful existence, working with his hands and following his creative inspiration undisturbed. Like multitudes of potters through the ages, through his ceramics he left marks of beauty on the planet. How many of us can claim that distinction?"

8
The Shopping List

"Shopping," Kabir thought, "has become such a basic part of being human. You just cannot avoid it." He needed a few things and decided to walk to the shopping centre nearby. He grabbed some bags, put on his coat, and slipped his shopping list and a pencil into one of the front pockets. On the one side he had written down some items, like disposable batteries, Himalayan salt and balsamic vinegar. On the other side were a few reminders of other things he had to do.

It was quite a windy day, but Kabir thought a little sunshine might do him some good. Suddenly he remembered that he also needed fresh fruit. As he took the piece of paper from his pocket to add it to the list, a gust of wind snatched the paper from his hand and swept it towards the hill next to the shopping centre.

Kabir tried to chase it for a while, but soon realized it was futile. He was now close to a small park and thought he might as well extend his walk. He found a bench next to a children's play area and sat down. He started thinking about the lost shopping list and mused that it was a good example of how all opposites were always next to each other; losing the paper was a loss as well as a relief. A slight movement in the brain labelled as intention becomes a desire, which then needs to be pursued. The lost slip of paper had defined the actions to be executed and then later forgotten. The loss of the list just speeded up the process of making the future the past.

Kabir's mind wandered to his visit to a Zen monastery in Kyoto a few years ago. There was an old monk sitting very still on the marble steps, his calm face a picture of timeless contentment and other-worldliness. He undoubtedly had the ability to transcend time and space, and the limitations of all other earthly experiences. Kabir watched him for a while, during which time the monk hardly moved. Kabir wished he could talk to the monk but didn't know how to get his attention. Maybe he could present him with a gift and that would bring him back to earth. But he also knew instinctively that there was nothing you could give a person who had no desire for anything. You cannot entice someone who can transcend the play of dualities and is happy with the perfect present and the eternal now.

The playful wind brought Kabir back to the present for a moment. It was as if the wind was talking to him, whispering ancient wisdoms about inner power that was at the root of life and manifested as cycles that caused all the human drama of feelings, from happiness to misery. Kabir lifted his face to the wind and surrendered to the now. Since his visit to Japan, he had also learnt how to leave the physical world behind. Mimicking the monk, he lost all sense of time and space and awareness of his surroundings. He basked in the inner stillness and absolute oneness that is the mother of everything that exists.

Then he felt something tugging at his coat. It was a little girl, probably only three years old. "Why are you sleeping here, Sir? This is not a bed," she said with a heavy lisp and ran away to her friends. Kabir felt rested, as if he had indeed been sleeping. For a moment he forgot why he was sitting in the park and how he got there in the first place. He looked around and saw two women preparing mangoes for their children. Fresh fruit! His memory sparked and he mused into thought, pondering that all human desires were like the shopping list, it will vanish in the winds of destiny.

Kabir searched his pockets and found a small notebook. He tried to remember everything that had been on the list and one by one he recalled each item. For now, he was in an earthly body bound by the earthly concepts of space and time and for now he needed to go shopping.

9

The Banana Farm

With her healing hands Jane came into my life when she was in her early sixties. She was a good reflexologist and had many stories to tell. I looked forward to treatments, just to hear her life stories. Some of the wisdom she had gathered was to avoid false expectations, as well as presumptions about others. She believed one should not take people at face value, because they are much more complex. She explained to me once that people often change unexpectedly, and that one should not be surprised by that.

Jane grew up in the Johannesburg of the 1930s, a vibrant but rough place even then. When Europeans and others descended on the city of gold, numerous factories sprung up to provide work for the thousands of immigrants. For every few who were materially successful, there were hundreds who were destitute. Jane, the only daughter of Welsh immigrants, fell somewhere in between. Her father had a job at a mine and her mother worked as a housekeeper for some of the wealthier neighbors. Jane enjoyed school; she was bright, hardworking and enthusiastic, and was looking forward to a happy future. Her boyfriend, William, was doing well as a maintenance man in a garment factory. He had a small car and the two of them loved exploring the city and its surroundings. Just before doing her matric, Jane fell pregnant and they married hastily.

It wasn't long before William lost his job and became a casual worker. During a holiday visiting family in the Lowveld, William fell in love with the easy pace of life and the awe-inspiring nature. He came across a small banana farm that was to be sold at an auction. With the help of a cousin, he bought the farm. When he enthusiastically informed Jane of the family's new future, she laughed nervously and when she calmed down, she held William's hand, looked into his eyes, and said, "I don't think my fingers have touched soil more than a dozen times and even then, only briefly." But William, very happy at the prospect of a new life for them, dismissed Jane's fears.

Although many other families in the area managed to do well with farming bananas, it proved more difficult for William. The first year required very hard work and was more costly than expected. Jane had no choice but to help and her fingers had to touch soil many times a day. She became quite the handy-woman, learning how to do basic plumbing and electrical maintenance, and even building cupboards. She also had a dozen coffee trees, which provided her with a small income. She loved the fragrance of the coffee flowers.

Within a few years some of the banana plants started to produce fruit and the future looked promising once more. Jane was fully occupied with housework, motherhood and another pregnancy. She also kept the accounts and made sure the dozen workers were looked after and performed well. By that time William had unfortunately acquired the habit of drinking alcohol, mostly a potent local brew. At first Jane ignored this development, but within a few months she noticed that he was often rowdy and very moody.

She began to write her memoir, starting with how surprised she had been that some people imagined farm life as being a wonderful escape from the rat race. For her it was far from idyllic. For six months a year the risk of fire was real and the thatched cottages could burn as fast as match sticks. Then there were the climate dangers. Hail was a seasonal fear, wind was a regular threat, and drought could bring disaster. Not to mention a wide variety of pests. The human factor also had to be considered, the unreliability of laborers, theft and delayed payments. She wrote about the illusive human desire to find paradise on earth and questioned people's optimism regarding finding a perfect life on earth. A Johannesburg newspaper started to serialize her letters and a small income trickled her way.

By the time her two kids were six and four years old, Jane couldn't cope any more. William had abandoned all hope of creating a sustainable living. He would stay in bed most of the morning and was now a confirmed alcoholic. They divorced and Jane moved back to Johannesburg with no idea of where and how she would make a living. She enrolled at a secretarial school and was quick to learn shorthand typing. At twenty eight she found a job as a bank clerk.

In an attempt to find some meaning in her life, Jane began to look at alternative religions and beliefs. She was drawn to the Theosophist Society, who happened to be promoting a seminar on alternative healing at the time, specifically reflexology based on Chinese pressure points. Jane took to it like a fish to water and in time she became a successful teacher of reflexology. She found the reduction of human pain and suffering a commendable pursuit that rewarded both the care-giver and the recipient. Her work with many clients showed her the correlation between a positive attitude and cheerfulness with a healthy immune system.

In her sixties Jane had one remaining desire – to visit her old farm again. She was pleased to learn that her old house was one of a dozen cottages in a health resort on the sprawling banana farmland. The owner of this resort invited her to stay in the house for two nights. It was during the last night of her stay that Jane penned the words that would become her mission statement in life.

"As your inner intentions are, so your life experience will be. Think good, speak good, and act good and you will experience goodness".

10
Zoo Lake Celebration

*From ancient times, human beings imagined
a state that was beyond pain and pleasure
– constant bliss.*

We all love to celebrate, to go out and have fun. Unfortunately, in some cases, celebrations can go wrong or even end up in disaster.

Young Solly was the star of a small Indian family who ran a grocery store in Johannesburg. Like many of his family members, he had studied accountancy at Witwatersrand University. When he was still a young man, his father died of pneumonia, leaving Solly as the head of the family. The family looked up to him to take care of business, as well as arrange family events and celebrations.

One of Solly's dreams was to take his grandmother on a boat ride, as she had never experienced it before. So, one day everything was prepared for an outing to Zoo Lake City. Many dishes were cooked and packed to take along. Solly arranged three cars to pick up the delighted family members.

When they arrived, several boats were already on the lake. They managed to find a boat that could accommodate all seven of them. Solly proudly allocated seats to everyone, but insisted that his grandmother sat next to him. Soon, however, the merriment subsided, as they realised that nobody really knew how to steer the boat or use the pedals properly. Solly was clearly not the captain of this boat. Predictably, the boat capsized and sadly his grandmother disappeared into the unforgiving water.

After much shouting, struggling and diving into the lake to look for their grandmother, they had to face the possibility that she had drowned. No trace of her could be found. About half an hour later, six soaking wet people emerged on the side of the lake. They stood there for a moment, shocked and silent, just staring at the lake. Then one of them slowly pointed a finger toward the water – it was the grandmother's walking stick floating gently on the water.

At that moment Solly hoped to die or just disappear forever. But he collected himself and went to report the accident and also to find people who could help search for his grandmother. After a few hours her body was found quite a distance away from the spot where she fell into the water.

The family and friends of the poor grandmother were immensely downcast and tried to find a reason for this terrible tragedy. They all believed in God's kindness and generosity. They just couldn't understand how God could allow this catastrophe to happen to the grandmother on her very first boat trip. It was supposed to be a celebration, but instead she left them. Did this mean that God had forsaken them?

> *Whatever concerns you at body, mind and heart*
> *level is given great importance and prominence*
> *– we are creatures given to exaggeration.*

11
Isabel in Salzburg

After the harrowing bombardment of Salzburg there was a day of calmness. Half of all the buildings in the city had been reduced to rubble by the Allied Forces. The early morning sun spilled its rays of hope upon the scene of devastation. Max was making his way cautiously to Market Square with its elaborate baroque fountain. Most of the buildings in this area were now in ruins. He found a broken bench, sat down and started playing his cello.

Max was a well-known figure in musical circles, especially when Mozart and Haydn were being played. A gentle breeze blew dust from the piles of rubble towards him and with the breeze and the rising sun, the stench of the dead animals intensified. He took out a red silk handkerchief, fastened it around his head to cover his nose and mouth and resumed playing.

Two figures were passing at the other end of the square. A mother and her young daughter were clambering over the rubble. The young girl, in a tattered grey frock, began to pull her mother in Max's direction. He acknowledged his unexpected audience with a nod of his head and continued playing. The beautiful little girl looked at him attentively. He stopped playing and looked at her sad face, haunted with fear and fatigue. The girl smiled and said, "My name is Isabel, and I am twelve years old today. What is this music you are playing?" "I am playing a requiem for the dead," Max replied softly, "and celebrating life at the same time. Do you like it?" She nodded, her eyes filling with tears. Isabel's mother took her hand and told Max they were making the difficult journey to the other side of the city to celebrate Isabel's birthday with family. Gently Max took Isabel's hand and wished her a happy birthday. Mother and daughter began walking again amongst the debris and the suffocating stench. A little tabby kitten emerged, meowing desolately. Isabel picked it up and asked her mother's permission to take it with them.

Three years later Isabel was a promising student at the Music Academy and played in a concert to celebrate Max's eightieth birthday. Afterwards Max gave her his red silk handkerchief and said, "Whenever you need to escape the never-ending distraction of this world, just cover your face with it and disappear into harmony and bliss." Isabel found this odd, but she treasured the handkerchief nonetheless.

Isabel married Zaki, a successful tax consultant. They had two children and Zaki, who enjoyed his material successes, often took them for holidays to the Caribbean Islands and ski resorts. When the children had still been little, they immigrated to Canada and enjoyed a good life there, although Isabel did miss her family. She was particularly sad to hear that her favourite uncle, Ignacio, had died. Ignacio was a Jesuit monk who was the last to leave the monastery after it had been sold to a hotel group. He then joined Albert Schweitzer at his leper colony in the Belgian Congo. This experience had disappointed him deeply and Ignacio died broken-hearted.

Isabel often remembered her uncle's last words to her before he left for Africa. "Be patient, for it will take you forty years before you begin to experience lasting contentment beyond pleasure and pain." She thought that she only had a few years to go and the contentment was yet to come. By this time she was an unfulfilled housewife with a husband who was a good man, but quite obsessed with wealth and worldly pleasures.

She decided to visit Europe to show Salzburg with its beautiful mountainous surrounds to her children. At the old Market Square they found a new museum and amongst the exhibits was Max's cello. She couldn't hold back the tears. Her children were baffled by their mother's sudden sadness, so she told them the story of how she had met Max. They wanted to know whether she still had the red handkerchief. "It must be somewhere," she said.

Back in Toronto Isabel started a journey of spiritual seeking. She also turned her house upside down looking for the red handkerchief and was delighted to find it in a box filled with her childhood memorabilia.

She had heard of a Turkish Sufi group visiting the city and decided to attend their concert. The chanting of litanies and the Shaykh's melodious voice enthralled her so much that she decided to join a Sufi group. She found a mentor and immersed herself in the new teachings. She came to understand that the litanies were like a ladder that helped her to ascend above the realities of the earthly realm. It reminded her of Max and how he also used music to clamber out of the rubble of the reality of war.

Zaki tried to be understanding, but being a rational materialist, he could not understand Isabel's yearning for spiritual growth. He listened to her patiently and came back one day with a ginger tabby as a gift. The little creature brought Isabel immense joy. She named him Aslan, meaning "lion". She thought, "My faith is still a kitten, but it will grow to become a lion."

Her Sufi mentor once told her that we are like children in this world playing with pebbles; sharing, caring, buying, selling, giving, taking, until we become aware of the divine treasure within our own heart. Once you know that the biggest mine of diamonds is within you, you won't care for inferior gem stones anymore. Celebrating joy is good, but something better than that lies beyond all your experiences and pleasures. Earthly dualities remain our battlefield, until we experience life through the perfect lens of unity. The world of suffering can be the springboard to the ever-present divine. Human intentions and actions can be sublime or ridiculous, but when Sacred Presence is realized, we will experience infinite blissful moments. The purpose of life is to celebrate sacred Oneness that envelops and permeates all. Don't ever be distracted by anything else until you are able to experience this truth.

Isabel would remember these words when she felt overwhelmed by life and all its uncertainties. She would then take some time to switch off, laying down on a couch, with the red handkerchief covering her face, chanting softly. Sometimes Aslan would jump onto her belly and when he started purring, time would just vanish.

She often wished she could tell Uncle Ignacio that she had, at long last, found the treasure of true contentment.

12
Supernatural Leader

All dualities have their root in the original
Oneness to which they return – the perpetual One.

On one of my travels I met Shaykh Othman, who was a latter-day Sufi master. During the 18th century the Ottomans encouraged East European Muslims to propagate Islam and Sufism and bring the people of those lands into committed loyalty to the Ottoman Empire. Shaykh Othman's great grandfather was one of those who ruled over a small enclave of a few square kilometres ending by the sea. He ruled with an iron fist very effectively without being loved or popular. Our present-day Shaykh Othman was a product of the strong network of Rifai centres dotted around East Europe. He was acclaimed by many of the present-day sufis as being a master of magic and miracles.

I was told by one of his followers that he had invited Shaykh Othman to a gathering at his house one evening during Ramadan. Another follower invited him elsewhere for the same evening, and he appeared in both places simultaneously, as had been witnessed by numerous people. Shaykh Othman carried an aura of non-worldliness and a power that overcame most other worldly powers. His extrasensory perception and ability to read the future was legendary. On certain occasions he was reputed to have put a spell on some undesirable people.

When I met Shaykh Othman none of these claims could ever be disputed as they had become part of his official biography. So all I could do was to remain on the side as an observer and marvel at some unexplainable events including the Rifai custom of piercing the abdomen using a sword, with no trace of blood. As I have the habit of not being too curious or absorbed in what does not make sense to the mind, reason or rationality, I let go of my link with Shaykh Othman and his followers, until some of them contacted me to inform me of a dreadful accident in Konya.

Shaykh Othman visited a saintly figure who lived in a small room on the roof of a very old three-storey building. The last few steps at the top had been exposed to the elements and some of them were badly worn. The Shaykh missed the last step and toppled down all three flights to the ground. He remained in a coma for a week and when he died, he was buried with much pomp and ceremony. Hundreds of his followers managed to reach Konya in time.

One of his close followers reached out to me and asked what I thought of the amazing stories of miracles and other unusual events surrounding him. My answer was that I was simply not curious about strange worldly events since I'm still in amazement of the miracle of life itself, and how it shines the light of consciousness upon time and space and whatever appears as a moving shadow.

I ended my connection with these people by praying for intelligent seekers to be struck by the all-encompassing divine Light before they leave their bodies. I think that seeking that Light is our duty and responsibility to ourselves and to our Creator.

13
Samandari Baba

*Everything that we experience is one of many
beams of light that permeates the universe.*

Samandari Baba, or 'he who is close to the sea,' grew up in Kashmir in a well-to-do family.

One night he had a dream in which a voice told him that he owed his life not to his family, but to the Life-giver, his Creator. Shortly afterwards a wandering dervish came to his town whereupon Samandari left his pregnant wife and followed the dervish.

Some years later he settled outside Karachi on the shore of the Arabian Sea, about ten kilometers from the latest housing development of the Defense Society. There were no roads or habitation of any sort. Within a week of living in a shack constructed of some orange crates,

Samandari Baba had a vision of Imam Ali telling him to prepare for the future by building a mosque on the shore. He started collecting stones from the surrounds and one of his friends donated some bricks and cement. After a few days the Defense Authority heard about this person squatting at a location that they considered to be too close to their land. They decided to send a high-ranking officer to enquire about Samandari Baba's purpose. The colonel told him that the land belonged to the army and that he would have to leave. Unperturbed, Samandari Baba told him that he was there under higher instruction to build a mosque and that the army should help him, rather than try to stop him. The colonel just laughed and while stroking his moustache, reiterated his command that Samandari Baba should leave as soon as possible.

A few days later the colonel ended up in hospital with intense abdominal pain. His wife, who was a very pious person, asked him if he had done something that he shouldn't have. She thought that he might have been cursed. At first, he couldn't think of anything, but soon remembered the squatter whom he had asked to leave. He told his wife where he was and when she found him, she asked him if he had cursed her husband. Samandari Baba denied this and assured her that he was simply following God's will. The colonel's wife promptly arranged for the delivery of the building materials required for the mosque, and her husband made a full recovery.

Within a couple of months, a beautiful little mosque materialized on the shore of the Arabian Sea. Samandari Baba kept the mosque locked to visitors; he was very clear that it should not be desecrated by the likes of the pompous army officials. He kept the mosque immaculately clean, sweeping every day and polishing the marble, waiting for a worthy person to come.

Within a year many people discovered the eccentric man, still living in a shack, surrounded by a few cats and two helpers. Even though the mosque was several kilometers off the gravel road leading to the nearby town, he got by with the bare minimum.

Samandari Baba had a very special connection with a few other people in Pakistan and India who could also connect telepathically with other people. I was visiting him once and while we were talking, he lifted his hand, signaling me to be quiet. I realized that he was receiving one of these messages. After a minute he said there were some visitors coming that he didn't want to see that day. We got into his old Jeep and drove along the shore for some time. Upon our return we learnt that some army officials had been there, wanting to pay their respects to him. He really didn't like anyone from the Defense or any other authority and was pleased to have avoided them.

I remember a conversation with him when we talked about how people bring about their own demise. He quoted from the Qur'an that God declared that He never wronged anybody, but that people wronged themselves.

He once received a signal from the unseen from a person hundreds of kilometers away. The person communicated to him that water was desperately needed in his area. Samandari Baba gathered some people to help, travelled there and oversaw the drilling of a well. The well provided good quality water, which eventually led to agricultural projects in the area.

When all the work concerning the well was done, Samandari Baba, to everybody's disbelief, said that he would die there. The very next day he sat down beside the well and died. He was buried next to the well.

The greatest treasure is the human soul as it reflects divine attributes. It is most rare in the sensory world but shines in the unseen.

Samandari Baba's reputation as a seer spread far and wide, especially after his death. Stories of his supernatural insight and visions of the future were told and retold.

The mosque is now in the middle of a built-up area. It was taken over by the Ministry of Islamic Affairs and opened to the public as a place of prayer. It is a gift to humanity that Samandari Baba's life story was written down.

14
Father of the Turks

Mustafa Kemal Atatürk was Macedonian, but he had always identified with the Anatolian heartland from which the Ottoman Empire had sprung. Anatolia would play a large part in his career, particularly Ankara, an unimportant Anatolian town, which he transformed into the capital of the new Turkish Republic. It was a stroke of genius to transform a poor town in the middle of nowhere, with a name originating from the trade in angora goats, into the capital of the new Türkiye. It was his way of circumventing the opposition from Istanbul. Slowly he built Ankara into his power base, while living modestly in the stationmaster's house.

Kemal had adopted many girls and brought them up as his daughters. He even employed a Swiss lady to teach them European manners and fashion. And my Turkish friend, Mithat, is the son of Iman, who was one of these girls.

Mithat told me that he had been privileged to learn much about Kemal from his mother, not just the man as a successful soldier and statesman, or as the father of our nation, but also as a human. Most people remember his public career, but not many know that during the latter part of his life he had adopted several girls of different ages and background and brought them up as his daughters. This was a surprising decision for a divorced man in a conventional society. He particularly adopted girls because he believed that if Türkiye was to take her place amongst the civilized nations of the world, the emancipation of women was essential. He paid for one of his adopted daughters, Sabiha, to train as a military pilot in a time when women in Türkiye barely stepped outside the confines of their homes.

Kemal came to political power after World War One, when the country was under the direct influence of outside powers. Yet, for all of his achievements, he drank and smoked heavily and did not seem to have much happiness in his personal life. His mistress committed suicide and his only marriage ended in divorce.

He was a patriot whose main objective was to salvage what he could of the defunct Ottoman legacy and build a new Türkiye that would take its place with pride on the world stage instead of being a country that was called the 'Sick Man of Europe'. He believed that Türkiye could not be led into the modern world when the nation's constitution was based on having a ruler who was perceived as the heir of the Prophet Muhammad and God's representative on earth.

By the early twentieth century intelligent Muslims had been wondering, if Islam was the correct path, why the Muslim world was in such a mess, individually as well as nationally. A few thinkers concluded that the problem was not Islam and its teachings, but the manner in which the Muslims historically formalized and organized teachings of the Prophet Muhammad, turning a path of living correctly and vibrantly in this life in preparation for the next into a list of outer prohibitions and regulations. One of the most important rules under the Ottomans had been to obey the ruler of the time, however debased he may have been. Senior imams would issue religious judgement at the death of the old ruler, justifying the murder of all potential claimants to the throne except for the new sultan. This was done on the grounds that having only one heir would save the country from potential civil war.

Although Kemal may have considered orthodox religion to be detrimental to Türkiye's modernisation, he was not without some inner faith. During the 1922 War of Independence he insisted on reciting the Qur'an during the evening gatherings with the commanders. He also sought the support of the Bektashi Sufis early in his political career, visiting the shrine of the Order's founder, Hajj Bektash, and dining with the then head of the order, Cemalattin. The latter supported Kemal's national resistance movement.

Kemal knew the old ways had to go but did not seem to have any spiritual nourishment to fill his inner vacuum. He would literally drown his sorrows in drink. Dancing, smoking and drinking were escape valves in a life dedicated to pulling his country, the bulk of who lived as if they were still in the Middle Ages, into the twentieth century.

In the summer of 1934 Reza Shah, the leader of Iran, visited Türkiye and was affected by Kemal's zeal for modernisation. Therefore Kemal indirectly had a strong influence on Iran. Reza Shah tried to base his modernisation of Iran on the Turkish model and looked up to Kemal, who had dispensed with the veil and fez, so Reza Shah banned the veil in Iran, too. There is a story that when Reza Shah and Kemal were travelling by train to Izmir en route to Istanbul they stopped at a place called Usak. Kemal was very annoyed to see a local mufti at the station wearing a turban, so he pulled the turban off his head. Later, he learned that this mufti was known for his enlightened views, so he sent him a present as an apology.

Hijab had become embedded in Iran as a sign of respect for among women. Whereas Kemal was successful in disposing of the fez and veil in Türkiye, that aspect of modernisation backfired badly on Reza Shah. The mullahs and religious leaders were part of the fabric of society in Iran. In the end it was easy to dispose of Reza Shah, because without their support his power base was flimsy. His son, the last Shah, had reigned for several years and did much for women's rights, but he was eventually deposed by a popular revolution, many of them chadored women. The irony is that the previous generation equated the veil with oppression, but for the Iranian women of 1979 it was a sign of pride in both their national and Islamic identity.

Like many other practising Muslims I had considered Kemal as the man who had put the final nails into the coffin of the Ottoman Empire, turned Türkiye into a secular nation and outlawed the Sufi tariqas. Imagine my surprise when, one day in New York, a Turkish Sufi Shaykh told me that he prayed for Kemal every day. He used the metaphor of an almost dead vine that had not been pruned for years and needed to be cut down in order for new growth to appear. It might have seemed that Kemal had chopped off the head of established Islam, but in reality he only disposed of the dead branches to allow new ones to grow.

How little we know if we judge events only against the backdrop of the time they occurred, rather than seeing their impact stretched over many years.

Now let us look at the issue of Mustafa Kemal being the 'The Father of the Nation.' The search for a father is the search for our origin, a search for security, for connection and for continuity. It was necessary for Türkiye, as it was reinvented, to have a new father to replace the figurehead of the Caliph. Kemal believed that he was destined for that role. He had this sense of destiny from early on in his career. One of his youthful inspirations was the nineteenth century Ottoman patriotic poet, Namik Kemal, who had written:

> *The enemy has pressed his dagger to the breast of the motherland.*
>
> *Will no one arise to save his mother from her black fate?*

In December of 1919, at the beginning of his political career, he recited this poem in the steppe town of Kirsehir in Central Anatolia. On this occasion he announced to the crowd that another Kemal had now sprung from the nation's breast, and changing the verse slightly, said:

> *Even if the enemy presses his dagger to the breast of the motherland,*
>
> *A man will be found to save the mother from her black fate.*

He repeated the same verse at a meeting of the Grand National assembly in Ankara and with that Kemalism was firmly on its way.

To this day many Turks believe that he paved the way for the successes of future generations and earned the right to be called the Father of the Nation.

15

The Necklace

The Yacoob family lived comfortably in a wealthy area of Durban in South Africa. Mr. and Mrs. Yacoob were happily married and felt blessed to see their children prosper.

One night there was a burglary at their home. Their large safe was broken into and relieved of all its contents. Mrs. Yacoob was inconsolable and couldn't stop sobbing.

A month later the local pawn broker sent a message to Mr. Yacoob informing him that a retired police officer had brought in an intricate Indian gold necklace weighing over half a kilogram. The broker had bought it from the officer for one hundred thousand rands and contacted Mr. Yacoob, who immediately offered double the amount just to get the necklace back. He placed the necklace in an ornate velvet box as a surprise for their wedding anniversary, only two months away. This necklace had been his wife's wedding gift and he couldn't wait to present her with it again.

Sadly, his wife had a stroke after receiving news that one of their sons had been in a motor car accident. After a few days in the hospital, she passed away.

Mr. Yacoob was heartbroken. For an entire year he visited her grave daily, sometimes taking the necklace with him. He spoke to her and told her about the necklace that was waiting for her. He asked her if she could come to him in a dream and tell him what to do. On his last visit to the graveyard, he held the necklace in his pocket with one hand, while wiping his tears with the other, and whispered, "No one deserves to wear this necklace, except my Fatima."

One night she appeared in a dream, wearing the necklace and radiating light. "If I had known how wonderful it was where I am now," she said, "I would have died years ago. Do you think that I need the necklace or anything else in my present state? Save yourself, dear husband, from all earthly illusion before it is too late."

Human migration is from material concerns to energies and light. Our journey on earth is towards eternal boundlessness and perfection of the divine.

16
The Failed Sufi

It was a peaceful afternoon in the British countryside with the flowers of late summer in full bloom. Steven and I were sitting in the drawing room of a beautiful classical Georgian house. The magnificent garden made for a lovely view, but our pleasant surroundings did not reflect Steven's mood.

Steven was an accomplished writer and his books had been translated into numerous languages and reprinted many times. He had also been born into affluence and enjoyed the lifestyle it afforded him; drinking and philandering were an integral part of his life.

He was reminiscing about his childhood at his family's house in Crete. It had been a few years since he had visited Crete. It was difficult for him to get away from his devotees and students, and

The Failed Sufi

he also had the habit of taking an extended retreat over the summer months.

He suddenly got up, fetched a file from his desk and threw it onto my lap. "Can you please read these letters between my Shaykh and me and tell me what went wrong?"

He left me to browse through the file. It soon became clear to me that his Turkish master had realized that Steven was not going to give up drinking, drugs and womanizing. The letters expressed the teacher's futile attempts to convince Steven to subdue the self and let his soul lead. When he returned to the room, he looked at me expectantly, eyebrows raised, waiting for my answer. I knew I had the answer, but that it was not the answer he wanted to hear.

Carefully I spelled it out to him. It was quite obvious that the Shaykh felt that the leaks and cracks in Stevens's pot would not hold the nectars and the perfumes that he had been pouring into it. I used the Shaykh's own words to try and get through to him, "Grace must overflow after your own cup is full."

Steven was visibly upset by my response. When he regained his composure, he pleaded his righteousness with me, "But my cup is always full, I've always been a happy and cheerful person!"

At that point I had to steer the conversation in another direction. I told him that the soul's expansion and overflow can only take place after the restriction and constriction of the lower self. I pointed out to him that his talk of cheerfulness had been superficial and related only to the lower consciousness and was therefore not sustainable.

After contemplating my words, Steven began to realize that his lack of discipline and obedience to his Master was indistinguishable from the cracks and holes in his vessel. Yet, he was still looking for a way out. He changed the subject by referencing the Highest, saying, "God is all-forgiving, so why is it that humans are not?"

I couldn't help smiling. "Dear Steven," I said, "God's business is His business, and your Master's business is his. They may relate and connect, but don't mix them up."

> *The soul is ever-perfect and the self is like a*
> *shadow desiring perfection, which can only be*
> *attained by perfect submission to the inner master.*

17

Meccan Sisters

Salman, an Urdu speaking man in his forties, had developed a reputable business by leading a group of pilgrims to Mecca annually. It was apartheid South Africa in the 1950s, where the Muslim migrants were mostly small traders, artisans or working the fields. After several Hajj trips, Salman had decided to move to Saudi Arabia and settled in Jeddah, where he became a well-known pilgrim's guide. He had clients from South Africa, Mozambique and Tanzania.

Shortly after his relocation, his daughter, who stayed behind in a Johannesburg suburb with her family, suffered a heart attack and died. She had three little girls who were now in need of care, because their father had been away most of the time, working in the mines. Salman arranged for Latifa, Najma and Ameera to relocate to Jeddah to live with him. He also had another house in Mecca, barely a hundred meters away from the Kaabah. He was part of the community of servants for the house of God, who also had a strong relationship with the merchants carrying all kinds of products from the East and West. The girls particularly loved the perfume bazaar.

By the time Najma and Ameera were both teenagers, Latifa, the oldest, was a beautiful and graceful woman who had learned the Qur'an by heart. She could also teach most aspects of the religion. The girls were the pride and joy of their grandfather.

Then, all of a sudden, their perfect world came tumbling down. Salman died unexpectedly and within a week the girls had to leave their Meccan home and go back to Johannesburg.

Back in South Africa, the girls were shocked by the Western habits, rampant drug addiction, and the hostile urban developments. Azaadville, with its temples and mosques provided a safe enclave for Muslims and Hindus, away from the Western life. The girls battled to learn English and to catch up on basic secular education. They found that many of their peers had already been positioned for professional careers in the outside world as accountants, lawyers or doctors. The girls had basically grown up in a medieval atmosphere, which they had enjoyed. But now they faced an immense challenge because they did not fit in anywhere.

Najma decided to become a teacher and was trained in the Montessori method of education. She opened up her own school and incorporated religious teachings in the curriculum. The school was a great success, with its cheerful atmosphere and frequent competitions in singing and recitations. The parents even began to take an interest in what the children were learning, especially regarding good conduct and appropriate behaviour.

The changes in new South Africa were rapid and the role of women changed radically. In Jeddah and Mecca, women assumed that they will be looked after, protected and respected. Not so in Johannesburg with its buzzing nightlife, bars and other shady entertainment activities.

Latifa was recognized as a pious religious teacher. She began to dive into the esoteric and deeper aspects of religion. She ran a weekly class for teenagers to demonstrate the universality of Islam and the inner meaning of the Qur'an. However, the success of her school came to the attention of some business sharks in Azaadville, who began to demand protection money from the three young girls who didn't belong to any specific clan or group. Most of their relatives had dispersed or passed away. Ameera joked that their tribe had decided to return to paradise because she could count more than thirty of their relatives' graves in the cemetery.

After eight years, the girls decided to move to Pretoria. There they were welcomed by the small Muslim trading community and soon Najma's school was full. She couldn't take more than forty children though. Again the parents realized that their children's experience of Islam was very different from theirs.

The stress of living in a world without any real support from the community began to take its toll on the young women. Ameera was severely depressed and almost bedridden. In Najma's school there were eventually only eight children left as the parents complained that their children could barely cope with the secular school curriculum and did not have time for the religious teaching as well. She had to close the school and began to shift her interest from children to birds. Latifa was diagnosed with breast cancer. Her joints began to swell and after being confined to bed for more than a month, she died. Although they had received very few visitors at their home, there were surprisingly many people at the burial.

Amongst them was a young lady who had claimed to have been a student of Latifa's, and as the body was being lowered in to the grave, she gave a brief obituary. She said Latifa had spent her life showing others that this life was only a prelude to an ever-lasting state that comes after death. She sang a few lines with an astonishingly beautiful voice.

I am a soul, a sacred soul ... a pure soul ... a heavenly soul. My body and mind are given life by the soul and is here to experience the world before its return to the cosmic Master.

"Latifa is now liberated," she said, "while we continue our struggle. May we too learn the harmony of surrender and peace before we lose all will."

The beautiful eulogy filled Najma with renewed energy. She turned their house into a bird sanctuary. Several peacocks arrived from the neighbouring farms until there were twenty-seven of them. She named each and every one and ignored suggestions that she could sell some of them. She believed that they were like us and the rest of creation – all the guests of the Creator, therefore worthy to be welcomed with an open heart.

18
The Allure of Sufala

*Worldly wisdom, plans and projects are different
from heavenly and spiritual wisdom.*

Since the discovery of gold it has attracted people like magnets and many lives are still lost today in efforts to find a little bit of this precious metal. Roberto was no different, gold always had an allure for him.

Many years ago he headed a well-known Spanish charity foundation in Zimbabwe. There he helped the extremely poor miners who had been scattered around the countryside, eking out an existence with gold panning. He rented out to them simple mining tools, like picks, axes, shovels and barrels at a low rent, thereby improving the quality and quantity of gold they mined.

Since he was already in Africa, he decided that it would be a perfect time to investigate the gold story of the ancient port city of Sufala in Mozambique. He knew that as far back as the Middle Ages Sufala had been known to be rich in treasures, especially gold. The gold wasn't produced in the area itself, but rather it trickled down the continent to the port from numerous locations stretching deep into Africa for hundreds of miles. It is most probably where the town got its name from; Sufala means 'lower down'. It was always overflowing with tons of gold, ivory and other sought-after commodities. The collecting points in this flow of gold were called 'zimbabwes,' meaning houses of stone. Today's famous Zimbabwe Ruins was only one of the larger versions of these fortresses where the gold carriers would settle for the night or deposit the gold for storage, for a hefty price of course.

The idea that the biblical legend of Ophir may have originated from Sufala interested Roberto, because most of the old references to this rich port pointed to southeast Africa, Tanzania and Mozambique specifically. In the early 20th century the governor of German Tanganyika, Carl Peter, wrote a book that became very popular wherein he attempted to prove that the area had once been rich in gold. Numerous discoveries of gold ornaments and relics had encouraged the idea of Ophir being in Mozambique or Tanzania. It is no wonder that the Portuguese tried to hang onto their Mozambican colony for so long.

Roberto decided to travel to South Africa first to meet with Shaykh Juma, a Sufi teacher who knew everything about Sufala and its history. The Shaykh told him that Sufala had dwindled to a tiny hamlet and that the natural port, which had operated for centuries, had silted over leaving most of the old ruins buried under the sand. He also laid to rest the myth that Sufala was rich in gold. Although it was true that some gold had been found in the sea, people didn't understand that it was transported there from all over Africa, from hundreds of little miners who found tiny amounts of alluvial gold in their areas.

The Shaykh also told him that the actual secret of Sufala was something entirely different: Shaykh Abdallah, a great saint, had been buried there centuries before and his grave was now at the edge of the sea, whereas before the silting it had been quite a distance from the ocean. Shaykh Juma asked his nephew, Yusuf, to accompany Roberto to Sufala to explore it. He asked them to spend their first night at the shrine of Shaykh Abdallah to pray and ask for guidance.

Before sunrise at the shrine, Yusuf had a vision of Shaykh Abdallah instructing him to go into the water in the direction of the sun for twenty meters or so, and then dive. There he would discover a sunken boat with most of it planks missing, but which contained a lot of gold. The Shaykh also told him in the dream that after hauling out the treasure, their first duty would be to build a retaining wall next to the shrine, which was about to disappear into the sea.

Sure enough, Yusuf and Roberto began hauling out several gold nuggets of various sizes. After two days of satisfying pickings, a few locals began to get curious and they had to cut their operation short. That same day they decided to leave with what they had. In their rush they had forgotten Shaykh Abdallah's instruction about erecting a retaining wall for his shrine. They boarded a chartered flight with the gold and took off towards South Africa. Just before take-off the plane dipped to one side and the wing hit the ground. After several minutes of heroic attempts by the Somali pilot to steady the plane, there was a sudden rupture in the wing. The plane crashed and all on board lost their lives. Hundreds of gold nuggets were scattered around the cactus and sisal fields.

Not long after the crash Mohamed Bakr, a popular Qur'an reciter, followed by a few locals arrived at the scene as though they had been waiting for the crash. He told the locals that he had had a dream of Shaykh Abdallah the previous night telling him to come to the area because they would find what they needed there to build a retaining wall for his shrine.

19
Abdul Jabbar – The Sangoma from Mozambique

It was a very special day because we were hosting a mystic from India, a venerable old gentleman known for his piety and healing abilities. We had gathered to greet the distinguished visitor and to have the honour of praying with him. Among the group was Abdul Jabbar, a gardener from the north of Mozambique, who had arrived at the farm under unusual circumstances, hoping to be employed.

Soon after Jabbar's father died, he appeared to him in a dream and ordered him to go to South Africa and find the people who pray towards Mecca. The story became even more bizarre when the boat he had taken to South Africa capsized due to bad weather and he was swallowed by a whale, which spewed him out on the shores of North Natal. His claim to be a modern day Jonah was difficult to accept, but then this fellow was no ordinary man. He said that his father still guided him in dreams. It had been on his father's instructions that he walked from Natal to find us and ended up working in the garden. The farm manager took him in on probation, but found some of his behaviour quite odd, such as his habit of talking to birds and wild animals, and embracing trees.

It was a crisp winter's day in the Lowveld of South Africa and we had decided to pray on the veranda, enjoying the warmth of the midday winter sun. When the prayer was finished, both Jabbar and the visiting sage walked to the entrance of the veranda, exchanging glances. We could see that their attention was focused on a palm tree nearby. Jabbar spoke little English, the Indian visitor none. Jabbar lifted his right arm with his index finger pointing halfway up the tree, and then moved his arm slowly up towards the sky. The sage performed the same gesture and said, "They have left."

Someone asked our visitor what had just happened. "There are wandering spirits," he said, "who only appear in remote deserts on earth, but today a few have visited us here. Jabbar and I saw these celestial beings mounting their heavenly horses and flying off."

A few months after this remarkable incident Jabbar volunteered to accompany me to visit some caves in the Legogote Mountain, which can be seen from our orchard, because I had heard that it had been an important meeting place for sangomas for centuries. On special occasions night long ceremonies would be performed there.

The day we chose for our five hour hike into the heart of the mountain started bright and clear. But by the time we had started climbing, rain began to hinder our progress. After a few precarious hours, sliding and slithering on the rock face, we reached our destination. The area around that particular spot had been cleared and was immaculately clean. It felt like a sacred place. As we were walking towards the nearby cave, Jabbar suddenly stopped and started to tremble as though he was in a trance. He bent down on his knees and started digging in the leafy soil with his strong hands. The earth had been softened by the downpour, and he soon managed to dig a couple of feet deep.

He shouted with joy as he pulled a beautifully bound Bible from the earth. With a trembling smile, he handed it to me reverentially. It was a very old Bible in which many passages had been underlined with black, red or yellow ink. A few feet further Jabbar started digging again and produced a carved short black stick and proclaimed that he was instructed to give it to me so that I can benefit from its mystical power.

Jabbar's unusual paranormal abilities helped a friend of mine who lived in Johannesburg to purge his restaurant and home from the undesirable energies left behind by the previous owners. Jabbar strode into the restaurant and headed straight towards one of the sofas. He plunged his hand behind the upholstery and plucked out a ball of black material covered with pins. Inside it were odd objects like buttons and small stones. "Didn't I tell you," he said, as he pulled out the offending article, "there are negative forces at work here." He then proceeded to the planters, took a small axe from his bag and started to demolish the concrete behind the planters. After some digging, he unearthed a small plastic eagle with a broken wing, and triumphantly offered it to my startled friend. He insisted that the cleansing wasn't done; he had to inspect my friend's house as well. With his amazed mother and brother as witnesses, Jabbar pulled out cloth bundles stuffed with pins and stones similar to the one found in the restaurant from various obscure places. Jabbar filled a whole tray with these objects, even breaking into the ceiling to find more. He refused any payment for his services, but said he would come for lunch whenever he visited Johannesburg, provided they did not serve him any pork. The restaurant turnover improved after this exorcism.

Back at the farm the other gardeners started accusing Jabbar of stealing tools and other objects left on the grass or in flower beds, but in Jabbar's mind these objects belonged to no one if they were abandoned outside. His room was chock-a-block with all these found items and rats and mice were running in and out from under the door. Needless to say, he was not well-liked by the other workers due to his behaviour that did not fit in with their culture.

One day, without a word, Jabbar disappeared and has not been seen since. He had often said, "I am in transit in this world and will soon return to the divine abode."

20

El Millonario

Outside the old village of San Jordi in Mallorca you can often hear the intermittent ringing of bells as a flock of sheep passes by. Sometimes you may see an oddly well-dressed shepherd leading the flock. He is a well-known wealthy local man known as The Millionaire, or El Millonario.

A few decades ago, his father had owned a big olive orchard close to the shore. As the tourist industry developed in the area, the big family farm at the seashore became very valuable real estate. The Swedish, known for being passionate sun seekers, favoured the millionaire's land and ended up buying most of it. Before long a hundred villas with magnificent sea-views were built there.

Dozens of old orchards and farms were sold to property developers for holiday homes and other tourism needs. As a result, the millionaire's generation ended up living in luxury in mainland Spain. However, El Millonario, whose real name was Ricardo, much preferred to continue sheep farming and producing high quality cheese.

Ricardo had studied economics at Barcelona University and had even worked for a financial services firm in Madrid for a couple of years. There he fell in love with an American girl who had dabbled with cocaine, and he was soon drawn into a nightmare of addiction. After two years of utter turmoil and often on the brink of suicide, he returned to San Jordi.

Soon after his return he went to an old monastery that had been converted into a rehabilitation centre, for a month. The treatment was successful. His remaining family welcomed him back and shared the good news that his share of the family wealth had been invested in a trust controlled by his uncle.

Ricardo converted a part of the farmhouse into an apartment where he kept a collection of Don Quixote Books. There were more than 600 volumes, some so tiny you could barely hold it in your hand. He developed a routine which consisted of waking up with the sunrise, doing Zen exercises, milking some of the sheep and having a small breakfast of his own homemade cheese with garlic and olive oil. Then he would lead the sheep to the open spaces and woodlands around San Jordi for grazing.

On several occasions I enjoyed a chat with him, surrounded by the chiming of the bells of the sheep. Ricardo also had a pet fox that roamed wild most of the time, but it would show up at his doorstep regularly for the food that he prepared especially for him.

He was indeed a millionaire in the truest sense of the word – having escaped the harsh business world with its pretenses and hypocrisies. Instead, he was living in beautiful Mallorca, caring for sheep, carob trees and wild rosemary.

21
The Jewish Catholic Sufi

Zahra had the strangest sensation that Shaykh Jamal was talking to her directly. Impossible of course, as he had been dead for several years. She was listening to talks commemorating his life in the Sufi Centre set up in his memory. A Jewish rabbi, who had often visited him in his last years, was trying to convince the largely Muslim audience that at heart he had never ceased to be a Jew.

"Well, Zahra," Shaykh Jamal seemed to be saying, "I can see nothing much has changed here. The idiots are still trying to put people in boxes. Perspective is very different from where I am now. A great relief it is, too. I was always difficult to box, wasn't I? It caused me no end of problems throughout my life. You wanted to write about my life, didn't you? But after a session or two I was tactless enough to die before completing my story. So, I am connecting today to tell you how it was …

"My mother was Jewish, so I was born a Jew. My twin brother died when I was twelve. My grief was so overwhelming that I turned to my paternal uncle for some sort of understanding why these tragedies happen. He was a Roman Catholic Bishop and that's how I became a Catholic. It was that faith that kept me going in the aftermath of my loss. Then I became a priest, studied law at Cambridge and ended up working in the Vatican. No reason to suppose at that juncture that I wasn't going to rise up in the church and become a bishop. But God's plot is greater than anything we can imagine.

"Watch it when you think you are on a clear trajectory, Zahra, because nothing is quite what it seems, and there really is an invisible hand that guides our destiny. We are given just enough freedom to think we have free will, but on issues that really matter we are in the hands of our Creator. The trick in life is to align ourselves to our destiny, whatever that may be. I like to think I did that, but it was quite a bumpy ride.

"My training as a priest was much more interesting than you might imagine, due in part to my inspired superior. As part of the course he sent me off to France to study. I had to lodge with two prostitutes and sleep in their living room. Of course, the clients would practically fall over me en route to the bedrooms. They were really kind women and if my superior had intended to teach me a lesson in humility and not being judgemental about stereotypes, he certainly succeeded.

"Out of the blue the Office of the Vatican appointed me as Papal Envoy to South Africa with the mission of deciding whether the church there was ready for a black bishop. And there was another rather embarrassing issue for the Vatican to investigate there: why my predecessor had converted to Islam.

"Once I had settled in Durban I decided to investigate the Muslims and find out what tricks they had used on my predecessor. I came across a group of Muslims who were active in calling people to Islam. One of them, Abdullah, knew the Bible well and used it in his drive to convert people of Christian background to Islam. I made numerous visits to him, telling myself and my superior all the time that I needed to fully understand those cunning Muslims' tricks. One time Abdullah invited me to visit an orphanage with him, which was situated out of town. He insisted at the time of prayer that I made wudu (ablution) and prayed with him. I was so deeply moved by this experience that I repeated it later that evening in the privacy of my own room. The feeling was the same. I was left with no option, I went to Abdullah and said my shahada (testimony of faith). The Church was not amused, to say the least. I was thrown out, excommunicated and left South Africa. As much as the Muhammadi light had touched my heart and a spark had been lit, it was some years before it was really ignited.

"I settled in Canada, where I had joined a successful law practice, got married and had a daughter. Finally there was some personal fulfilment and happiness. Islam was a part of my life, but more background than centre stage. Then tragedy struck. My wife, who had been a champion skier, and my young daughter travelled to Europe to attend the Olympics. They were both killed in a car accident. 'Why,' I cried to God, 'is everyone I love taken from me?' The black cloud of depression overwhelmed me and sickness weakened me. My life seemed over. It was the wisdom and guidance of my local imam that saved me. He counselled me to return to South Africa, where I had first experienced the Muhammadi light, and start again there.

"Back in South Africa, I embarked on years of study of Qur'an and Arabic. I came like a baby to Islam and had to learn all the rules. The grounding I received during this period was to act as a launching pad for my later spiritual journey. Also, I became a proper 'pukka' Muslim; adopted the dress, ate like the Indians and suffered from the chilli foods, but sometimes got rewarded by Ayesha's fruit cake. She soaks it in orange juice instead of brandy. But no one understood my particular British sense of humour.

"The South African Indians were kind and accommodating to converts, especially when they realised that I actually knew the Qur'an. The Arabs, well they are another bunch. Arrogant creatures, they think no one who isn't born Muslim is anything other than second grade.

"Years of teaching and living amongst the Muslims followed. When I started preaching, it was by the book, with a lot of concern about the outer rules and regulations. As a Catholic priest, I loved the poetry of St. John of the Cross; the Spanish mystic who had been inspired by the Sufis of Muslim Spain. Very few of the priests I knew talked about living with the light of Jesus in their hearts. Suddenly it was not enough to just be a good Muslim and follow the rule book. I wanted more. So it was to the Sufis I went for the final part of my spiritual journey.

"As destiny would have it I had been introduced to a Sufi master who asked me to review a draft of a book about Happiness in Life and After Death. This manuscript transported me to my ever living soul. It also took me out of the ethnic and limited boundaries of structured religion. Next to that book, it was you, Zahra, who caused a crack in that tortoise shell we call self or ego. I was full of traditional concepts about women speaking in mosques. My chauvinist Catholic background had been replaced by an equally chauvinist style of Islam. Then I heard you talk in a mosque about the Qur'an and its impact on your life. It touched me deeply. The blinkers were off. In a way you were an unwitting actor in the drama of my road to transcendence.

"Health issues and pain dogged my last years on earth, but there were countless blessings too. As my outer world shrank, so my inner world began to expand. Some of my friends couldn't understand my new liberated attitude, although I was in no way denying the importance of following the basic laws and regulations of Islam. You don't put a young sapling in a field and expect it to grow. First you contain it in a box, once it has grown you plant it in the open. If you keep it in the box it will not yield fruit.

"I had a rich life, along with all its trials and tribulations. Few people can claim to have been a Jew, a Christian and a Muslim. What a blessing to be exposed to the full spectrum of the Abrahamic family. Don't pay too much attention to that Rabbi though, he is a well-meaning bloke and he did offer me a place in a very upmarket Jewish old age home.

"Just remember, Zahra, there is no point in living unless you take the journey I took from ignorance to knowledge, from darkness to light, ever seeking the limitless zone of the soul within. Remember too that with every difficulty there is a double ease. Take the challenges of this life as a chance to refine the ego-self. Islam is about submission to whatever there is for you at the moment. Do your best, but accept that in the end there is only One Controller."

Suddenly the voice faded and with a start Zahra came back to the gathering. By then the Jewish rabbi had given way to a Catholic priest. She smiled as she remembered the indomitable spirit they were all commemorating. He contained within him all the teachings, had travelled down many roads, traversing them with his own particular brand of humour. He had been impatient with hypocrisy, but had sincere affection for the sincere seekers who had crossed his path; a great being fondly remembered by many.

22
Cleopatra's Carpet

Dimitri's gallery in Piraeus, Greece was filled with antique items and objets d'art. These items were not really museum pieces, but rather targeted at a specific clientele, namely individuals who believed that these objects could help them transcend time and place. The price tags were, of course, quite exorbitant.

I accompanied a friend there once. He was an American collector of spiritual relics and had been in contact with Dimitri for a few months before our visit to arrange a viewing of three specific items that he was interested in. Around midday we arrived at the gallery, situated next to a large olive orchard. We were greeted at the door by Dimitri, looking very flamboyant with his long black hair clasped in a ponytail. He escorted us to a dimly lit corner where the objects were laid out on a table. He assured us that these articles carried intense sacred messages and could transport whoever was holding them into the field or energy that they had last been exposed to by their original owners.

The first item was a small piece of carpet, worn at the edges and obviously restored. The colours were faded and the pattern of the weave could no longer be discerned. It was claimed to have belonged to Cleopatra and to be from the same carpet she had been concealed in when she was rolled out in front of Julius Caesar. Dimitri told us that the piece of carpet had come to him from one of the custodians of the last remnants of Greek relics of Alexandria. It had been lying in bank vaults in Switzerland for the last century.

The second item was the shirt that Imam Hussain, the grandson of the Prophet Muhammed, had been wearing when he was slain in the battle of Karbala. All followers or scholars of Islam know that Imam Hussain was a fully enlightened human being with no fear or concern about anything. It is said that no one could hold the shirt for more than a minute without tears welling up in their eyes. To our amazement that was exactly what happened to us, which of course just increased my friend's interest in it. He was overcome with emotion and in a trembling whisper asked, "How is it possible that a piece of cloth can bring the emotions of an incident that occurred fourteen hundred years ago?"

"I don't know," Dimitri said, "but a man with such intense faith like this Imam is like an extraordinary actor who jumps out of a tenth story window with total confidence that he is going to fall on a safety net on the other side. It is beyond courage and beyond our understanding of timelessness."

Dimitri then relayed a story about how Napoleon, whilst campaigning in Egypt, became interested in Imam Hussain and Islam. "He was disappointed because he couldn't find a Muslim teacher that impressed him. The clerics he had met were just strict followers of the theology and devoid of any light in their conduct. Even so, it is well-known that Napoleon took on the attire of the Muslims while he was in Egypt, dressing in the latest fashion. Some historians have speculated whether he actually converted to Islam, but that he was interested in Islam cannot be disputed. Apparently, he had asked several people to tell him about Imam Hussain and the event at Karbala. It is said that the shirt might have been offered to him at that time."

Lastly, a hoof that supposedly belonged to a donkey that carried Jesus in the Palm Sunday procession was presented. My friend, his eyes shining with delight, picked it up as if it were a delicate piece of porcelain. He commented on how he could see how old this hoof was. Dimitri nodded his head and was probably already counting the money he would make from the sale.

I was wondering whether I should tell my friend that I knew where this hoof came from. An acquaintance of mine from Iraq told me that his father had come up with the plan of selling hooves to American Christian churches at the beginning of the twentieth century. His father was an Assyrian Christian priest who had married a French lady. He saw an opportunity to supplement his meagre earnings by selling donkey hooves as Christian relics. Beirut antique dealers played a key role in his endeavours and soon he was selling one or two hooves per year. His swindle was discovered when these churches started holding annual conventions where all kinds of relics would be displayed. After a few years the people had realized that a few dozen hooves were in circulation. At that time there were shops that specialized in making any item look like an antique. They would sand it, burn it, let it rust or bury it in soil, and within a few weeks the 'antique' item would be shipped.

But I remained silent and decided not to trample on my friend's dreams. Dimitri, whose whole life revolved around finding these items, was absolutely thrilled at the anticipation of making another sale. And there was my friend, as happy as a child about the prospect of owning a supposedly holy hoof.

While the price was set and the transaction completed, I wondered why the love of objects of historical significance is so deeply rooted in the human psyche. The answer came to me clearly: we live in time but seek that which is timeless.

23
Journey to Healing

After trekking through the Atlas Mountains for two days, Margaret reached the village she had been dreaming of. It had been several years since she had had a vision of this magical place, perched on the edge of the Moroccan desert. It was a sanctuary nestled between two mountains, where a cascading waterfall welcomed the visitors to the shrine of Sidi Ismail.

Under the trees of the mausoleum's courtyard sat a circle of ladies swaying rhythmically while reciting a religious litany. Margaret approached the circle with caution, until one of the women beckoned her to join them. After they had finished their recitation, the leader of the group, Maryam, got up to hug Margaret and held her in a tight embrace. The other women spoke welcoming words and Margaret, suddenly overcome with emotion, burst into tears. She felt cocooned and nurtured by their warm, comforting energy; a feeling she hadn't felt in a very long time. In her broken Moroccan dialect she thanked them.

When her tears subsided, Maryam wiped her cheeks with her colourful scarf and made a place for her in the circle to sit down. She asked her why she was so deeply sad. At first the words just stuck in Margaret's throat, but after a while they came out, interrupted by bouts of sobs. She told them about how she was experiencing every mother's worst nightmare: her daughter had died. The loss was consuming her and her marriage also crumbled in the aftermath. Her husband just couldn't support her in her grief. Being all alone again in the world made her yearn for a new partner, someone that could lift the veil of sorrow and give meaning to her life again.

Maryam gently stroked her back until she stopped crying. Gently, she drew her head on to her shoulder and in reasonable English, whispered in Margaret's ear, "You are like all human beings, looking for liberation, but in the wrong place. All of mankind are in exile in this world. Our purpose is to acknowledge this eternal truth and find a way out, but not through another person or a new religion. We must forget about everything except our souls, which the Muslims call the 'ruh'. Did you know that 'ruh' also means 'to go' or 'to be a breeze'? The eternal light of the 'ruh' is a gift to all humanity. So we must all leave our earthly burdens behind us and focus on the heavenly souls within us."

The sobs subsided and Margaret stopped crumpling the handkerchief in her hand. She was calm now and finally had the courage to look up and face Maryam and the other women again. Maryam continued speaking. "As women we have great advantage over men. Women have greater compassion, patience and willingness to sacrifice. In truth, we are God's agents who perpetuate His creation. We are born wise, whereas men first need to get rid of their childishness before they can realize their 'ruh'. I have counselled hundreds of women in villages around here and it is always the same story. They all think that the right partnership will bring them fulfilment. I hear myself repeating over and over again that a successful marriage can only reduce your existential darkness, it can never give you light, for that is already in you. A good man or a good teacher can only show you how to remove your self-inflicted veils and shadows."

Silence fell over the women as Margaret contemplated Maryam's words. She looked up through the leaves of the tree to the clouds sailing serenely in the sky and felt as if a weight had been lifted off her chest. She took a deep breath and exhaled slowly. She pleaded, "Please tell me what I should do next. I cannot bear to go through the world with this dark hopelessness in my heart any longer."

"Stay here for a few days," Maryam said, "so that we can console you and you can find your strength again. Then you must go home without any expectations that happiness will come to you through another person or any external factor. Islam has taught me to live in the moment. This always takes me back to the eternal spot in my heart, my 'ruh'. You have the same 'ruh' and can access it too."

Margaret started crying again, but this time Maryam asked the other women to leave her be, because their new friend was crying cleansing tears, expelling the grief she had been carrying for so long. Maryam was right, the tears gave way to a sense of immense relief and tranquillity.

As the day was coming to an end, a few more ladies joined the circle and a noisy celebration started all around her. They began to sing a beautiful verse that Margaret did not understand fully, but she could make out that it was about the path to Paradise that will be given to us when we are truly bereft and have given up the quest. And that any concern or awareness of other than the One will surely bring grief and confusion. When you cry for God and He answers you, He strips you of your past and holds you in the basket of His mercy.

After some time back in England, the elation she had experienced in Morocco wore off and Margaret's depression returned. She constantly remembered the tragic death of her five year old daughter. Endlessly she relived the fateful day when she rushed with the child to catch the school bus. The small hand had slipped from her grasp and her daughter had darted across the busy road and was run over by a truck. She never ceased to blame herself for her thoughtless rushing and impatience on the day of the accident. Once again she spent her time weeping or sleeping, refusing to be numbed by the medication the doctor had prescribed. She was exasperated because it felt as if she would never get better.

One night, after waking up from another nightmare, she got up to warm some milk. While waiting for the milk to make bubbles, she wondered at her own impatience, while God was so patient with His creation. She thought of the women in Morocco again and prayed that she could rediscover the peace she had experienced there. The milk and her exhaustion helped her to fall back into a deep sleep. This time there was no nightmare. Instead, she had a vision of her daughter smiling at her and saying, "It is only my body that died, Mother. If you can silence your mind, you can still see me in your heart. I look far prettier now and don't even need to steal chocolates." For the first time in a year Margaret woke up with joy in her heart and began to sing a couplet that came instantly upon her:

"It is my impatience that has lifted me to God's infinite patience. Oh, You, Who have made me, it is only You who can save me from me."

In her mind she was transported back to Morocco and the presence of Maryam. She could feel Maryam's welcoming hug and she knew then that for the rest of her life she would experience this magical link with the wise Moroccan woman.

24
The Man on the Mountain

The modest mausoleum of Ibn Mashish, a great Sufi saint, in Chefchaoune, Morocco, is perched three thousand feet high on top of the Atlas Mountain, like an eagle's eyrie. The spectacular vertical drop to the valley below has taken away many a visitor's breath. The area is forested with cork trees and the surroundings of the tomb are carpeted with a thick cushion of cork bark. For many years the shrine could only be accessed via a very narrow dirt road. This trek through the dense cork forests had to be undertaken on foot, which could take up to two days, or with mules, in which case one could do it in about six hours. Nowadays the road is wider and paved.

Many years ago a friend and I undertook the expedition to Ibn Mashish's tomb. The road had been widened and was being prepared for asphalting, so we had an easy start, but the wind suddenly changed direction, fog rolled in and then it started snowing. As soon as the snow hit the road, it melted and our little rented Fiat started to slide on the narrow, muddy road. We were not discouraged and continued our precarious ascent with a very steep drop looming on our left-hand side. "Well, you know the tradition," my friend said, a bit nervously, "Pilgrims to Ibn Mashish's shrine are always challenged by difficulties and obstacles."

We were not too far from the top when a figure appeared out of the thick fog waving a hand for us to stop. By then it was snowing heavily and the car was sliding bravely in the fresh mud. It was a young man, clad in a thin nylon shirt and dripping wet. As I rolled the window down, he peered in and asked if we had a cigarette for him. It was such a strange and unexpected request under the circumstances that I did not respond. I just turned and looked at my friend, who told the man that we were non-smokers. The man was clearly disappointed and shook his head with an air of bemused puzzlement.

At that time, it had become frustratingly clear that our car was not able to climb any further and we were forced to slide back slowly the way we had come. We knew about another longer but gentler route and decided to give it a try. Hours later, utterly exhausted and freezing cold, we found ourselves a few meters away from the same spot where we had to turn around. And ... there was the young man still standing where we had left him, waiting for us. We invited him to join us.

Ibrahim was a member of one of a handful of families claiming to be descendants of Ibn Mashish. He lived a few hundred meters from the shrine in a small hamlet and he often talked to the dead saint. He told us that some people referred to him as the Holy Fool. With his help and the mercy of the abating snow, we eventually reached the shrine. After getting out of the car he said, "You really have to make sure you have cigarettes in your car when travelling." Bewildered, my friend reiterated that we did not smoke and were really quite against it.

The man's shirt was soaked in the drizzle and I felt guilty for not realizing before the sorry state he was in. I got out of the car, opened the boot and retrieved a warm cashmere sweater from my suitcase. I offered him the sweater and some money. He smiled in a way to acknowledge the gifts, but also as to say, what can I do with these?

On our way back after visiting the shrine, we saw Ibrahim again, standing near the same spot that we first met him. Without the sweater. We stopped to say goodbye. This time he knew not to ask for cigarettes, but he said that we should visit his spiritual sister who lived in the huge cemetery in Cairo and that we should tell her that he had sent us. He told us that she lived in one of the underground tombs and we would see how similar, but yet different, they were. "I talk to her as often as I talk to Ibn Mashish," he said. "She has great healing powers and always helps people who ask for her help."

A few days later when we were crossing the desert south of Marrakesh, an army lorry sped past us, spraying up clusters of sharp stones. Within minutes steam rose up from the engine and we had to stop. After the arduous journey up and down the mountain, the little Fiat now had a hole in its radiator. Our only option was to ask for help from any vehicle that might come along. Hours ticked by before our rescuer showed up. He inspected the radiator, smiled and said, "Only cigarettes can help you now!" My friend and I looked at each other, eyebrows raised and had to admit, once again, that we did not have any. He went to his car, brought back a packet of cigarettes and ceremoniously emptied the tobacco into a container of water. He let it stand for a few minutes and then poured it into the radiator. "The dry tobacco leaves expand in water and as they circulate around the radiator they will plug the hole. This will at least get you to the nearest town to have it fixed," he explained.

As we were witnessing this, I could almost see the man on the mountain pointing at us and laughing. I felt quite embarrassed for judging him outright without bothering even once to attempt a sincere conversation with him. Just one simple question could have saved us from a very long afternoon in the desert.

25
The Woman in the Grave

I was part of a small group visiting Sitt Nafisa's shrine in the necropolis of Cairo when a woman approached us. If I had to guess I would say she might have been in her fifties, but she looked ageless. Her plain long-sleeved cotton dress was well-worn. She asked us if we would like to see the tombs at night. She added that she would accompany us on this special tour. We were very intrigued by this unusual offer and everyone immediately accepted.

We started with the recently renovated marvelous mosque and shrine of Ibn Ata Allah al-Iskandari and proceeded to visit a few other famous Cairo saints. This all happened in the dark with a very small torch as our only light.

Remembering the tale of a woman who lived in a grave in Cairo relayed to me by the man on the mountain in Morocco, I asked her where she lived. I was starting to think that our guide was the same woman. "Right this way," she said and led us down some steps, still deeper into darkness until we entered a fairly spacious underground tomb. Judging by some sparse bedding items on the one side, it was clear that she often slept there. Someone asked her how she managed to make a living and she told us a fascinating story. Whenever she needed any money, she just asked her master, held her little bowl in the corner of the tomb and dozens of coins would drop into it. She would instinctively know when it was sufficient and would say 'bas', meaning enough. She showed us some of the Egyptian coins, which she mostly used to help others.

I told her about the man whom I had met on a mountain in Morocco, and she was ecstatic to hear it. "How marvelous, he is just like me!" she said. "We both spend more time speaking to dead saints than living people, because, well, they are just more alive than most living people!" She could not contain her exhilaration and started to sing this song:

> *The ocean is one ocean*
> *but the fish and their colours are countless*
> *The Creator is only One*
> *but His creation is beyond measure*
> *We are all from Him and by Him will return*
> *and whoever knows this is already in the ultimate perfect destiny*
> *and whoever does not, help them and remind them to understand.*

An hour or so later, still stumbling in the darkness, we were heading towards a new mosque and a shrine. According to our tomb dweller guide, he was the last of the saints to be buried there. When he was still alive, Shaykh Abdullah had been a successful building contractor who spent most of his wealth helping and feeding people and he had also been the patron of the thousands of grave dwellers. He had died the year before and the next morning would be the anniversary of his death. Many people were expected to come and visit his mosque and they had to be fed.

As we approached the mosque, I realized that we had been at the cemetery for many hours. Night was slowly turning into day, and I became aware of two figures approaching us. Our guide reassured us that they were in fact bringing us an early breakfast; Egyptian bread wrapped around some freshly cooked meat and spices. They said that they had been preparing to feed the many guests who would visit the shrine at dawn, and that we were the first guests. I asked them how they had known that we were on our way. They replied matter-of-factly that the deceased Shaykh had informed them of our arrival and had implored them to go and feed his first guests.

> ***The ultimate miracle is timelessness in time,***
> ***mortality as a glimpse of immortality.***

While enjoying our breakfast, we felt immersed in an ambiance of kindness and love. For a few minutes I had an out of body experience during which I celebrated the intertwined nature of what is physical and what is ethereal and eternal.

26
Meshti

'Selfless devotion' – the two words that best describe Meshti, my adoring first nanny. She started taking care of me when I was only three months old, and her love for me was an immeasurable obsession. I was the centre of her universe. When I left for Europe at the age of sixteen to go and study there, she too departed. But I did not know it at the time.

She originally came from the Mazandaran province in Iran. Her village lay on the shores of the Caspian Sea at the border of Iran with Russia, an area famous for its caviar and walnuts. Her husband owned orchards, rice fields and a couple of fishing boats. It was a pleasant life lived in an earthly garden. Her son, Reza, was born after some years of marriage, completing her happiness. But within a short time Meshti's perfect world totally collapsed. Her husband was crushed between two boats during a storm and shortly afterwards she lost her baby to cot death. Within a month Meshti fell from paradise into hell. She suffered from paralysing depression. Her mother, Fatima, feared for her daughter's sanity and prayed for a solution to the crisis.

Fatima had been on an extensive pilgrimage the year before to the shrine of Imam Hussein in Karbala, Iraq, where we lived. She wanted to visit our family because she had heard that pilgrims from our native province were always welcomed at our house. There were always visitors at our house, and everybody was received with open arms. Some people, especially a few widows, even stayed if they had nowhere else to go.

Fatima also hoped that perhaps my family would help Meshti. It was arranged that a relative would escort Meshti to Karbala and take her to the house of Shaykh Ahmed, my father. It would have taken about a week to travel from the lush fields and forests of Mazandaran to the desert oasis of Karbala, a town which lived to commemorate the martyrdom of Imam Hussein and has one of the most visited shrines in the Islamic world.

A confused and grief stricken Meshti arrived at our house and my father gave permission for her to stay with the ladies in his extended family. As she entered the ladies' quarters, Meshti heard a baby crying. She rushed to the crib, picked up the baby and cradled him in her arms. That baby, was of course, me. Her empty life had suddenly found a purpose again and for the next sixteen years until I left Iraq that purpose was me. I was the same age as little Reza and all the love she had lavished on him was now mine.

Lovely Meshti, with her soft blue eyes and fair skin, translucent like opaque porcelain, became my obsessed nanny.

I took her love for granted. She was there at my beck and call, catering to my every whim. My earliest memories are of titbits that she sneaked out of the kitchen for me. Oh, the trouble she used to get into with the other ladies in the household with those disappearing fried onions and chicken livers! I became adept at communicating with her by telepathy and remember one day sending her a message to bring my favourite soap to the bathroom. She came with the wrong type of soap and, of course, I sent her back for the right one, the green olive variety from Damascus.

In our large household Meshti had to live with various other ladies, like Nana Sakina, who was jealous of her and made her life difficult. Umm Hussein was easier to deal with, as was Umm Rahim, who was a bonesetter. There were many visitors and a lot of kitchen work. When she wasn't looking after me, poor Meshti had to work over open fires and kerosene stoves. She had been used to a more genteel way of life in a moderate climate and so her sensitive skin broke out with eczema. She considered all of these sacrifices worth it to be at my side. Karbala became her home and she never returned to Iran.

By the time I was a teenager I remember her saying often that if I ever left Karbala to continue my studies she would die from grief. When the time came for me to leave for England on a government scholarship, Meshti was desolate. We had already left for Baghdad, from where I would take the flight to London and she was so desolate that she decided she had to say goodbye one last time, so she ordered a taxi to take her to the airport. That was the first and the last time she ever took a taxi.

Instead of driving her to Baghdad the driver took her to some small village about three hours away and left her there, where she was exposed to the fierce sun for hours. She only managed to find her way back to Karbala the next day. By that time, she had a high fever and probably suffered from sunstroke. She died before I even reached London.

But nobody told me the sad news. In fact, I was delighted to have found new medication for her eczema in London. I did not have much money as a student, but I would buy this ointment and send tubes of it home every two months, until my brother wrote to me and said that Meshti no longer needed it. I found this odd, but it was not until nearly a year later that I was told about her departure. I was preparing for my first trip back to Iraq and my family knew they could no longer hide the news from me.

The loss was immense. She was the first important person in my life to have died and no matter how many times we hear that death is just the next phase of life, at the time it was devastating to know I would never see her beloved face again. On the mantelpiece the half a dozen tubes of eczema cream that I had bought for her was a constant reminder of her departure.

The blow was softened somehow by the numerous encounters I had with her in lucid dreams. In these dreams she was in a wonderful state and always expressed gratitude for the way her earthly life had turned out. She could lose her ego-self because she had devoted her life to other human travellers. Her pride and joy was that I had been the last altar of devotion for her.

I will never forget dear Meshti. Her memory is proof of how our earthly experience and our souls relate to timelessness. The Truth is ever alive.

27

The Ramana holiday

Thoughts come and go. Feelings come and go.
Find out what it is that remains.
– Ramana Maharshi.

The aroma of freshly brewed tea filled the kitchen. While pouring the tea into her mother's favourite cup, the Noritake with the tiny yellow flowers and soft green edges, Beth wondered how she was going to convince her mother to join her for a much-needed holiday. She handed her mother the cup and asked, "Mother, when last have you been on holiday?"

"I hate holidays," Sarah complained with a furrowed brow. "People plan and discuss and look forward to their holidays and then return with tales of how much they enjoyed themselves. I know better.

When your father was alive, we also planned weeks ahead, but then something would always happen. We would lose something, or the weather would change drastically – once there was even a cyclone – and we would become annoyed with each other and disagree about everything."

Beth fidgeted nervously with her teaspoon and said, "Oh, Mother, it really couldn't have been that bad?"

"Really? Don't you remember that holiday when we had to leave early?" Sarah replied. "It was absolutely horrible! The neighbour in the next-door apartment was rowdy all the time, especially at night, probably on drugs, and the management didn't do anything about it. And a dog bit your brother! You know, even just the thought of going on holiday upsets me!"

"But, Mother, please …"

With her tea untouched in her lap, Sarah's beliefs about vacationing were in full flight now. "As for the usual talk about the pleasures of holidays, I know that most of it is heavily edited and make-believe. That is why before a photo is taken, people become self-conscious and try to look happy. A real holiday is one which shows you the best and the worst of yourself, like a magnifying mirror that reveals even the small warts and wrinkles you try to hide. No, no, I don't think I can ever have a relaxing or enjoyable holiday again."

"Mother, just please hear me out. I want to take you on a special holiday. You have been taking care of all of us for years and now you need a change and some rest. Just look how pale you are. I'm really worried about you; you fall ill so frequently these days. I know of a lovely place, tucked away in the mountains and only three hours' drive from here. The people there are kind and they will take good care of us. Please let us go, just you and me, we can leave everything behind for a few days and spend time with no worry or concern."

Sarah took a sip of tea. Her brow unfurled and the beginning of a smile touched her mouth. "Oh, Beth, I do love the idea of leaving everything behind for a change. Even though I know it might not go according to plan, it does sound exciting. I also expect that when the excitement is over, I might feel a bit depressed. But I do love the idea of a holiday with you, away from my boring daily routine."

A few years earlier, Sarah had thought that religion might help her to have a better life. After visiting several temples and churches, she had not found a convincing way out of her inner doubts and conflicts. While she did find some of the Eastern wisdom very helpful and palatable, the practical and structured aspects of most religions just rubbed her the wrong way. Once Beth asked her if she had ever followed a religion. She replied, "It is bad enough to have one, but I had several! We need a direction or path towards higher consciousness and certainty about life and death; and religions try to provide that outcome. But I now know that my soul is eternal, it is the source of my life and that is my universal religion."

On the third day of their pleasant, and thankfully uneventful, vacation, Sarah found a little book in the living area called "Who am I?" containing the utterances of the long departed famous Indian sage, Ramana Maharshi. The thin booklet was a reflection of how little he had spoken during his lifetime. Sarah read the book every day and found immense value in its teachings. In essence it held that if what you were looking for was not definable, discernible or materially visible, then what you were really looking for was the light of your soul, the true source of your life. To find it you had to stop the chatter of your mind, to stop everything and touch the timeless now. Once you master this, you will find yourself at the threshold of supreme consciousness, which is eternal and boundless.

She asked the landlady of the holiday home if she could take the booklet with her. Now, every time she looks back at her past, or a touch of sadness comes over her, she holds the little book firmly in her hand and effortlessly transcends her thoughts and the trap of conditioned consciousness to a blissful state that is better than any holiday she has ever had.

28

The Story of Hayy bin Yaqdhan – The Living Son of the Awakened

This is a story that you might never have heard before. It is the story of Hayy bin Yaqdhan, who was raised by deer on a deserted island.

This classical Islamic story was written by Ibn Tufayl in the twelfth century and became popular in European cultures. It has its origin in Andalusia in the south of Spain and has had an immeasurable influence on Western philosophy. It is believed that the concept of 'tabula rasa' – the human mind at birth as a blank slate – originated from Hayy's tale.

There are a few versions of the story, but essentially it is about a king who wanted to improve the quality of his people's spiritual practices and worship by asking Hayy, who was living alone on an island, to come and help them to reform their religion. Although there are many different interpretations of the story, it is generally believed that Ibn Tufayl tried to point out that if one is not in communion with nature, one cannot be in communion with life.

An interesting aspect of the story is that Ibn Tufayl provided two different beginnings, both explaining the origin of Hayy. The first one is more secularly styled and tells a story of a despotic king's sister who had a forbidden love affair with Yaqdhan, a man from a neighbouring kingdom, and gave birth to Hayy. Fearing her brother's rage she placed Hayy in a sealed box and put him out to sea. He washed up on a deserted tropical island where a doe heard his cries and took care of him. The alternative beginning is more religious and suggests a mystical spontaneous creation where Hayy grew from the earth. Some clay started fermenting and formed bubbles which took the shape of a human being whereupon God sent a soul to inhabit it.

Hayy lived on the island for fifty years before he ever met another human being. He grew up in the fruitful wilderness alongside other creatures without the influence of other human beings. Therefore his conduct was exemplary: he never destroyed anything that was alive and he only took what was needed to survive. Everything he needed to know, he learnt through observation, experimentation and reasoning. He learnt that when breath leaves the body, the soul also leaves and the body left behind is just a shell. As he grew older he realized that he was different from the animals on the island, that he could manipulate his environment to make clothes for himself or create shelter or weapons to defend himself. At one point he started staring into the sky at night and his spiritual awakening began. He grasped that there had to be a creator, a higher power that was in charge of life. Soon after he met Absal.

He had come to the island to seek solitude and to get away from his friend, Salaman. They differed about what was most important in practicing religion. Salaman believed that the content, symbols and instructions they had received from a prophet were sufficient. But Absal felt there had be some deeper more mysterious meaning and that one should contemplate this in a meditative manner.

Absal taught Hayy how to speak and was amazed at the pure truth that Hayy had discovered by simply observing the natural world around him and by using his reasoning to understand the nature of the universe. Absal and his people had come to the same insights, but with the help of a prophet. And the truth had to be recapped again and again by rituals and by surrounding oneself with images and symbols.

After much time had passed, Absal asked Hayy to accompany him back to his country, where Salaman had in the meantime been crowned as king. Absal wanted Hayy to impart to Salaman the pure truth that living alone in nature had taught him. He was intrigued by Hayy's insights and asked him to explain these to his people. Hayy, however, was astonished about what he saw in the town. Especially about how much people could accumulate: belongings like shoes and clothes, food, furniture, livestock, as if they would never have enough. He was astounded to see how of out sync they were with nature and how obsessed they were with their own personal survival and comfort.

Hayy started preaching at the mosque every Friday. He tried to make the people see that they were just passing through here on earth, awaiting the time when they would go back to the abode of the heavenly unknown. He implored them not to affect the natural flow of life by changing the ways of nature to such an extent that they become obsessed with material objects and easy living. He tried to teach them about inner reflection and the enlightenment that can be gained from it, the importance of being able to touch the zone of infinity within their own hearts. But every Friday fewer and fewer people came to listen to him. Hayy realized that they preferred ritualistic practice, material riches and the transient pleasures of life.

Hayy explained to Salaman that the people didn't want the changes he was trying to implement and asked permission to return to the island. He suggested that the king bring back the priest and the formal religion the people preferred. Salaman had to concede that Hayy was right. He asked Hayy if they could come and visit him on the island, but Hayy vehemently refused. He insisted that the people would ruin it, trying to make it the same as the town. He argued that the culture with its organized ways that Salaman was part of should not spread, as it would destroy the natural flow on earth.

In most versions of the story Hayy returned to the island with Absal where they spent their lives contemplating God.

29
Aziza Begum

Aziza was recovering from a long illness. After every prayer she would stay on her prayer mat to recite the litany, "Oh, Allah, come to my aid", four hundred times. A wandering Qalandari dervish had given her this prayer a few years before, while passing through her neighborhood. She invited him for lunch after she had spotted him from her upstairs bedroom window sitting on the pavement opposite the house.

Her husband was a wealthy textile manufacturer. After his death, his partners, who were also his brothers, bought her out and carried on with the business, only contacting her occasionally when social conventions required it. Her son, Amjad, was doing well as a professional engineer, but had little interest in his mother's welfare. He was besotted with his beautiful Afghan refugee wife, whom he had married in New Jersey and brought back to Islamabad. Not long after their arrival, Amjad's wife had developed a neurotic condition that caused her to faint unexpectedly with increasing frequency.

"Oh Allah, why couldn't Amjad find a healthy girl who would enjoy life with him and also be close to me?" Aziza would lament. She often talked to God, mostly complaining and asking for fulfillment of her wishes. One day she retrieved her large box of jewellry from the safe. Touching each piece tenderly, she wondered whether Amjad's wife would ever relish any of it as she had developed a vulgar American taste in all aspects of life.

At one point, Sikandarabad, the family village where Aziza had grown up, was flooded and many of her relatives had to be rescued to other parts of the village. But these parts also suffered mud slides and minor earthquakes. After the disaster, her cousin Naseem had come to visit and Aziza was very distraught to hear that Naseem's children and two maids had died when the house had collapsed over them. The farm lay below a muddy lake of water and all the cattle were either stolen or dead.

Aziza's thoughts wandered to her past and all the numerous family dramas and challenges. As tears welled up in her eyes, she looked through the window and couldn't believe her eyes. On the pavement on the other side of the road the Qalandari Sahib was sitting in the same spot as he had years before. She genuinely believed in his divine connection and his ability to tell the future. Sitting next to him in the house, having brought in sweetmeats and tea, she immediately launched her complaint that her supplications were not working anymore. She almost became angry when he expressed surprise and said that he had already asked God to accept her prayers. He lifted his arms with authority and proclaimed solemnly that all her prayers were already answered, but she might not be able to see it clearly.

He told her that it was her stray thoughts and lack of focus that had caused her confusion. Then he touched her forehead where the third eye is, pressed it with his thumb and asked her if she experienced light flowing in and out of that spot when she was in prostration. She sighed and said that she wasn't sure if she did. Assertively he said, "You have to work on that."

Aziza asked him about the village disaster and the ever-increasing requests for financial help from distraught relatives and friends there. She wanted to know what she should do about all the pleas for help. He smiled perceptively and said, "You can never save the world, for it will produce its own ever-growing shortages and earthly needs. But at least do what you can with what is in front of you. Give whatever you can to needy people, even if it means that you must sell your house and move back to the village." He then laughed and said, "I would like to see you milking the goats and eating rough millet bread." He told her that she might think that it would be going backwards but assured her that it was the best of futures, and that Truth was in the present, not the past or the future.

Aziza was shocked and wasn't sure what to make of this strange advice. Soon the answer became clear.

One of Aziza's numerous charitable acts was to support Salim, a distant relative, to go to university and complete his medical studies. After receiving his qualification, he came to visit Aziza to inform her that he had decided to go back to the family village and open a practice there. She took it as a clear sign that she, too, had to go back to her village.

Within three months an old barn next to Salim's surgery was remodeled as a cottage for Aziza. Ducks and chickens were competing with dogs and cats for her attention. And, to her great surprise and delight, during the first week of the month of fasting, Qalandari Sahib arrived at the village. He announced that he was going to break his lifelong habit of not staying in one place, and that the village would become his home.

When you discover that bliss that emanates from your own soul, you are awakening to the divine cosmic presence.

Aziza was very grateful to have a tangible cause to live for that thrived under her care. Salim's free clinic flourished and within two years several new buildings were added, including an orphanage, schools for boys and girls, and other public services.

Before she died, Aziza Begum was revered as the Mother Teresa of Sikandarabad.

Salim decided to compile a book of photographs and anecdotes on Aziza's life, combining it with the story of Sikandarabad's origin and history. Like several dozen other places, Sikandarabad claimed to be founded by Alexander the Great. He smiled at the thought that all people are looking for ancient origins and always yearn to go back to where they come from.

30
Futile Success

His climb on the ladder to political success had been tumultuous and marked by constant struggles. But when he eventually reached the top, his doubts began. He could not understand why his success failed to deliver on its promise of joy.

A publisher had already advanced the payment for his autobiography. It was to depict a thrilling picture of his upward climb with the usual omissions and changes. The new airport was to be named after him. His serious educational reforms and scholarships for disadvantaged students had made their mark. His close colleagues and supporters were full of admiration. Yet, he was not.

The seeds of doubt and disillusionment grew so rapidly that all the blooms that had sprung from his myriad of successes were dwarfed by weeds of uncertainty. He was afraid that the shadow of these new plants would overtake everything else and the garden of his dreams would wither and die.

He started reflecting on his doubts, but to his shock he discovered how insensitive those closest to him were to his inner conflicts. His daughter had even told him that her drinking problem began because of his neglect and the lack of love and care that she should have received from him. He had almost forgotten the dark night when she returned home from rehab. She had wept. He had wept. Even his beloved cat had left the room.

Over the years there were many friends who had let him down or had even become enemies. These numerous betrayals reached a crescendo just before his last political victory. Everywhere in the world political life is treacherous, but in his country it was warfare. Emotional volcanoes lie barely concealed below thin veneers of civility and friendliness.

He wanted out. He wanted to run from everything with all his might. But how? The real conflict was not how to leave the pinnacle of power, but how to do so without collapsing the entire structure. It is one thing to go into retirement, yet another to abandon a political party that you, yourself, had created. Only now did he fully comprehend the meaning of the saying: be careful what you wish for.

For the first time in months, he went to the local church, lit candles and prayed for guidance out of this cul-de-sac. He begged the Virgin Mary to come to his aid. "I know I chose this career, but now I need your guidance on how to disappear from it. All these entanglements have become meaningless. My desire to lead this country has disappeared. The battlefields I waded through have changed me irrevocably. In the beginning I was sure I knew who was friend and who was foe, but after the last battle I just don't know who was who and most of all, I don't know who I am. The ambition that has propelled my rise has totally vanished. I started with passionate competition and near the end I relished co-operation. Now I live in desperation. Mary, mother of Jesus, help me."

He sought counsel within his religious circle. The wisest amongst them said, "Keep praying and hope that you will be slowly excluded by the other fighters, so that you can allow yourself to be kicked out of the ring."

And so it happened that after a few months he was summoned to court. There were several accusations about his abuse of office. Embezzlement was amongst the charges brought against him. Yet, anybody who really knew him would tell you that he had no interest in money.

In the end he was stripped of office, and he returned to the church to give thanks. Prostrating himself before the statue of the Virgin, he cried out, "O Blessed Mother, I now have experienced utter humiliation, but at the same time relief from my worldly burdens. Thank you for shining a light to show me the path to get out of that world full of conflict and uncertainties. Thank you for helping me understand that life on earth is only a preparation for what will come after death. Blessed Mother, you have enabled me to live fully in this world and to be fully prepared for the next. Your motherhood is both earthly and heavenly. Thank you, thank you, thank you."

31
Pedro and Son

Pedro was my trusted gardener at our beautiful summer home in Mallorca.

He was incredibly connected to nature and had an intuitive understanding of the weather, fauna and flora. He had never left the island and also never handled any money, his wife Maria was in charge of that. The grass was trimmed by the few sheep he kept. The snails on the vegetable patch fed the ducks and the pigeons, producing luscious eggs and meat. The entire orchard was self-sustaining. One shed was kept for winter vegetables and was filled with bunches of braided garlic and baskets of tomatoes, onions, lentils, carrots, almonds and numerous types of beans. Pedro was especially proud of his small sweet sugar melons.

He grew up on a poor farm on a windswept rocky patch on the northeast of the island. My orchard, in contrast to his own, was an easy paradise for him to cultivate. There was no waste whatsoever; everything fed everything else. From the moment he stepped into the orchard in the morning, he just followed his head and heart and did the right thing at the right time almost effortlessly. He was constantly at work and hardly ever took breaks.

Pedro's only son was a university graduate and he had been immensely proud of him. That was until he married a very ambitious and demanding girl. She, too, was educated and constantly aspired to ever more luxury and a better position in society. Their daughter-in-law's attitude was an anathema to Pedro and his wife.

The son was desperate to please his wife, who was in many ways much stronger than him. She drove him to care too much about money and status. His job as a mechanical engineer at the airport didn't pay enough for her needs or desires. In an attempt to impress his wife, he started playing football for the island and was soon spotted as a rising star.

Pedro was very skeptical about his son's new career choice, and his wife realized that their son was drinking considerably more than before. Needless to say, the parents became very concerned about their son's health and well-being.

One morning, as the island team was playing against Sicily after heavy rain the day before, tragedy struck. Pedro's son broke a leg and sustained a severe head injury. After several days in the local hospital he had to be transferred to the mainland. Pedro's blood pressure shot up and he too had to be taken to intensive care for a few days. It was then that Pedro, who was quiet and accommodating all his life, called his daughter-in-law for a serious talk. This ended up in a shouting match and even higher blood pressure. His daughter-in-law then looked Pedro in his eyes and said, "As soon as my husband is out of the hospital I shall ask for a divorce. I know what I want in life and I will get it with or without him."

Pedro was discharged the next day. He came into the house with a large flat basket full to the brim with eggs, tomatoes, grapes, artichokes, melons, Brussel sprouts and onions. When I thanked him he said, "I have to thank you for giving me this wonderful paradise which makes me forget the rest of the world. My son will be coming out of the hospital on crutches soon and I feel sorry for him. This place on the island is a paradise, but the new generation is making their own hell and there is nothing I can do."

The natural parental hope is for their offspring to be better equipped for a happy life and a contented heart.

32
The Heartless Mufti

A few decades ago the first shelter for battered women was established in South Africa by a Muslim woman who had become aware of the magnitude of abuse against women which was a complex issue cloaked with shame, denial and fear.

When she was sixty years old, Ayesha sought protection at this shelter. It took a few days before she could tell her story. On the first day she had just sobbed, her body shaking from the shock of years of abuse. The next day, utterly exhausted, she just slept.

She described her childhood as being fairly pleasant, having had a kind father and a devoted, hardworking mother. But during the first week after marrying a hafiz, who could recite the Qur'an by heart and who was also the prayer leader of the local mosque, she knew that she was condemned to a life of servitude with very little sweetness or kindness. Their three children had grown up and were all living their own lives. Their attitude towards their mother unfortunately reflected the harshness of their father. She said that she found herself at a stage of her life where she wanted to make sense out of everything, but she did not know what her destiny was. The Qur'an promises that whoever lives his religion fully, will live well in this world and in the next, but she had certainly not experienced it.

It took many attempts for the social worker to convince Ayesha's husband to come to the shelter for a conversation. At first he was very resentful and resisted, until he was informed that he might face legal charges for the abuse of his wife. The next interview went better than expected, and he agreed that Ayesha could stay longer, until she wished to go home again.

Her ambitious husband was now a senior cleric and a mufti, always expecting obedience and subjugation. Many of the young trainees wished to learn from him. They, too, wanted to become mullahs, because it was believed that a family with someone who had memorized the Qur'an may be transported to paradise, therefore it was a great prestige to have one boy in a family to be selected and pampered to attain that status.

Ayesha was delighted to learn how to use a computer at the shelter and started learning the Qur'an and its meaning from the internet; and the more she learnt about her religion, the more she thought that some mullahs were very ignorant. She was surprised to find out about all the different religious groups and that some of them were very different from what she knew; many of them were much more moderate and tolerant. The emphasis was on conduct and improving quality of life. This appealed to her.

Ayesha eventually became a familiar face at the shelter, initially helping with food preparation. She was a good cook. After completing some online courses, she started counselling other battered women. She was especially good with the younger girls. Sometimes she remembered how she had thought there was no hope for her, and felt extremely grateful for the opportunity to give hope and life back to others. The irony wasn't lost on her – to help other abused women, she herself had to go through it first.

She did divorce her husband in the end, but being able to forgive him confirmed to her that she had found a new lease on life, filled with hope and blessed with kindness. In time she developed a healthy amnesia of her previous life.

33
Father Fey of Kirkuk

Father Fey, a prominent Jesuit scholar, had lived and worked in Baghdad since the 1960s. His interest in history and religion began in his childhood, where he spent hours in the library at the family chateau in Bordeaux. Soon after receiving his degree in history and anthropology from the Sorbonne, he joined the Jesuit order and went to Iraq.

He lived in a guesthouse dedicated to the Jesuit order where he occupied four sparsely furnished rooms. The house belonged to a well-known Baghdadi family, whose daughter Yasmin had been helping Father Fey with his work on a sporadic basis.

His bedroom was a square box and had a small window near the ceiling without any curtains. Near the entrance was a black steel bed and under the window stood a small wooden table and chair.

Underneath the bed was an old suitcase containing his clothes and other belongings. A rough cross made of two old twigs nailed together hung on the wall above his bed. This was the only decoration in the room. The bookcase was a makeshift structure of two wooden planks sitting on a pile of bricks, which supported several old books and manuscripts.

During the first few years there he completed his research on early Christian history, covering Northern Iraq, Syria and the Levant. His main specialization had been Assyrian Christians and after spending two years with the tablets and other relics of Nineveh he was awarded a doctorate of philosophy on the subject. He was also very interested in the development and spread of Christianity in the mountains of the north.

His publications had been very well received in the academic circles of history and religion. However, with the coming of the Baathist regime, the Assyrians, being close to President Saddam, had become quite influential and they disapproved of much of Father Fey's findings. His research proved that present day Assyrians in Iraq were not at all descendants from the ancient Assyrians, as they had claimed to be. In fact, they were from a different ancestry altogether.

He received several warnings from the authorities to withdraw his assertion regarding the present day Assyrian lineage. He tried to explain that these had been scholastic and academic findings and that it was not up to him to change them, but to no avail. By that time France had been sending fighter jets and numerous weapons to the Iraqi government, which were subsequently used to gas thousands of Kurds and kill countless Iranians.

The French embassy had been aware of the threats against him and advised him to return to France, as they were unable to protect him sufficiently in Iraq. One day he was summoned to the embassy in Baghdad, but on the way there his car exploded before hitting a big tree on the side of the road. Nothing came from the subsequent investigation and Father Fey was buried in the Christian cemetery of Baghdad with very little fanfare.

Yasmin was very upset about the suspicious way Father Fey had died and began an investigation, relying on her family name and influence. Her husband was a director of education in the government, but not even his membership of the Baath party gave him immunity. He was warned to stop his wife's pursuit of the fate of Father Fey. She seriously contemplated emigrating in order to continue her investigation, but that had proved unfeasible. She realized that her husband would lose his job and reluctantly she gave it up.

Yasmin turned her attention to all of Father Fey's papers. Some needed to go to Paris and others to the French embassy. She kept only one piece of paper on which Father Fey had written in ornate calligraphy, "What is out there in the world is already in your heart and that's how you perceive and experience anything."

Instead of obsessing over Father Fey's death, she decided rather to continue his work. She started to look into the history of early Christianity in other communities in Iraq and came to the conclusion that the mountainous part of the country provided badly needed shelter to the early Christians who had to hide from the authorities in Rome. For the rest of her life she did whatever she could to help visiting Christian scholars and others like them.

To accept natural and human limitations and boundaries is the first step towards awareness of the boundless within us – our soul.

34
Orlando's Farm

After the Second World War, British and German yachtsmen discovered the splendor of the northern coast of Spain with its numerous pristine beaches. The small town of Port de Pollença particularly caught their attention and within a decade it became a popular family resort.

Having inherited the family farm just about four kilometres south of the Port de Pollença, Orlando became a fifth generation landowner. His predecessors had practiced mixed farming with almonds, oranges, grapes, watermelons, as well as sheep. When his father was still alive about two thirds of the farm was sold to local developers. Soon the landscape changed. The orchards, vineyards and pastures made way for the Hotel Pollença Park and hundreds of apartments and villas sprung up. Orlando's family was left with about three thousand almond trees and a flock of sheep. He had little interest in farming, so when a German hotel group approached him to buy most of the rest of his land, he eagerly accepted. It was like a dream come true, he was now a wealthy man.

Orlando was a professor at Palma de Mallorca University teaching Philosophy but spent most of his free time pursuing his hobby, geology and island formation. As a child he spent much of his time climbing outcrops of rocks along the seashore, sometimes collecting mussels and crabs. This became his passion.

With his newfound wealth, he couldn't wait to acquire a large boat to explore the Balearic Islands and to pursue his hobby of exploring rock outcrops wherever they appeared on land. He also bought a small apartment in Bendinat further south on the coast for overnight excursions. Orlando was looking forward to many trips around the local coastlines with his beloved wife and daughter.

Orlando felt as if he was living in a dream. Almost every weekend was spent on the boat on the way to yet another spot on the coast. On one such a trip, the family stayed in Bendinat. While Orlando was helping his wife to prepare lunch, their nine-year-old daughter, Anna, played on the beach. She loved building intricate sandcastles and often got lost in her imagination, forgetting everything else around her. Orlando was sure she would one day become an architect.

The boat was anchored close to one of their favourite coves. Suddenly a freak wave pushed the boat into the air. It jumped meters through the air heading straight towards Anna. She was too absorbed with her sand sculptures to see it coming and the boat smashed into her. After two days in the hospital, Anna passed away.

Overcome with grief, Orlando decided to sell the boat, but nobody wanted to buy it. The apartment in Bendinat also remained empty for a long time. He sank deeper into his sorrow when his wife, unable to deal with the death of her daughter, had to be admitted to a psychiatric hospital.

Eduardo, the realtor, who tried to sell the apartment, befriended Orlando after the tragedy and became very concerned about his mental state. Eduardo was somewhat of a philosopher and believed that the day of birth should always be celebrated as a death, because we start dying the moment we are born. He gave Orlando a book by Ramon Llull, who had spent many years with the Sufis of North Africa and became Mallorca's famous Monk-Philosopher-Sufi. Underneath his statue in Palma is inscribed in Spanish, English and Arabic: "There is no merit in any action without love." Orlando would often pick up the book seeking solace from his grief, but for a long time none would come. After reading the book many times and reflecting on it he accepted his state of grief and melancholy. At the same time, he also started to understand that only unconditional love could end the illusion of separateness and otherness.

Many years later, during a lecture on Kierkegaard and existentialism, one of Orlando's students asked him to share the most important lesson of his life with them. The student said that though he found the professor's lectures very valuable, he thought that personal advice from Orlando's own life would benefit him even more.

Orlando sat down on his desk and went quiet for a while. He was trying to decide if he should answer the question at all. And if he did, what would he say? He knew that his response might influence his students more than any lecture ever could. He looked back at all the eager faces in the lecture hall, their eyes bright with anticipation, and decided that they deserved an answer. The University of Life is after all man's greatest teacher. He put down the book he was still holding, stood up and addressed his students.

"You all know that Kierkegaard famously said that 'Life can only be understood backwards but must be lived forwards.' When I was still a young man I acquired some wealth and I was very excited about it. I thought that it would change my life. Well, it did, but not in the way that young people imagine, that money would bring them happiness. My biggest desire was to spend as much time as possible at sea with my family. In those days I would have said my purpose in life was to drift along with leisure and pleasure, but I have found that the other side of these pleasures is grief and unhappiness. I have learnt the hard way that what you desire today may bring you disaster tomorrow. My daughter died and my wife lost her will to live because of my desires. That is the understanding my life backwards part."

Orlando hesitated before continuing. "I must confess to you today that the living forwards part still remains a bit of a puzzle for me. After the tragedy I kept looking for a door that would lead me to serenity, to certainty, to some guarantee that nothing will change so drastically again, which is of course impossible. I have yet to find lasting tranquility and peace. I do think I'm getting closer though. Recently I have spent three weeks in one of the rooms at the monastery of Lluc. It was there that I came to understand that there is another level of consciousness within us; a higher zone, if you will. It lies beyond our reason and intellect, but the demands of our daily lives make us earth-bound, and instead of acknowledging the heavenly creatures we really are, we chase happiness outside of ourselves. This is the life lesson I would like to share with you – love yourself enough to make time to explore that level of consciousness. It will connect you to the only certain thing, to the Source from where your soul's light originates."

35

The Palestinians

There is so much fear, paranoia and anger amongst many Muslims about anti-Islamic propaganda and attacks, both verbal and physical, on their peoples and their faith. At the centre of it all is a rallying cry against the decades of injustices perpetrated by the West.

Shaykh Jamal is a Sufi master who was born in Jerusalem and had lived in the Old City all his life. I thought he could shed some light on the situation. With this thought in mind I find my way to him, strolling through the markets of the Arab Quarter on a bright winter's day. The soulless developments of modern day Israel poised to engulf the Old City seem part of another world. Propelled back into some distant past I experience the stuffy, winding alleyways, the small cluttered shops with their windowless niches crammed with goods and the hustle and bustle of human activity. The spice market leads into the fabric market, which turn into shops selling brass and earthenware. In the small cafes men with the characteristic Palestinian chequered keffiyeh, worn as a headdress or scarf, sit sipping Arabic coffee or mint tea, discussing politics with the impassioned rhetoric so beloved of the Arabs; all caught in some time warp. The people in the streets with their different facial features and dress tell the story of Jerusalem, the Golden City. Here Bedouins mingle with those of Jewish, Turkish and Crusader heritage, while the tourists buy bric-a-brac from the black descendants of Ottoman slaves. Fair haired people with blue eyes can be seen alongside those of darker hue.

Through this very Arab vista runs the Via Dolorosa, the road walked by Christ to Calvary. An endless flow of priests, nuns and pilgrims continue to traverse its cobbled route, commemorating his crucifixion. A stone's throw away is the Dome of the Rock, built on the site of Solomon's temple, from which the Muslims believe the Prophet Muhammad made his night journey to heaven. Under the Dome is the rock-summit, where legend says Adam was created out of dust, where Cain killed Abel, and Abraham prepared to sacrifice his son, Isaac. On the Temple Mount is a footprint claimed by the Christians to be that of Jesus, and by the Muslims to be Muhammad's after their conquest of Jerusalem. A city sacred to three religions, Judaism, Christianity and Islam, has during its thousands of years of history been the scene of endless conflict and strife. Yet these three faiths have much in common: they all take the Prophet Abraham as their spiritual father. Centuries of cumulative human misery has given rise to a saying in the Arab Quarter when someone dies, "Jerusalem has killed him". The medieval Arab traveller al-Maqdisi wrote that "Jerusalem is a golden goblet full of scorpions".

I muse over all this while walking up the steep shuttered lane that leads to Shaykh Jamal's house. The door is open and I find him sitting quietly in the reception area amidst colourful cushions and carpets, surrounded by supplicants. They come from all walks of life to seek his counsel. The religious scholars like to engage him in debate on interpretations of certain verses of Qur'an. His close devotees request guidance on the mystic path. Business men ask him to pray for their commercial success; a mother for the healing of her sick child. An ocean of love, the Shaykh offers answers for their troubled hearts.

Shaykh Jamal intuitively knew the reason for my visit. He beckons me to sit by him and serves the mint tea himself, waiting for the other visitors to leave so that he can give me his undivided attention. "So much human tragedy, so many years of grief for our people," I say to him, "when will it ever end?"

"Human tragedies," he replies, "continue so long as there are human beings. There are two levels of tragedies. One concerns people as individuals, the other involves societies, communities and nations. When basic justice is violated, an individual is shattered because the root of that violation is lack of respect and love for the human soul. Injustice breeds in the darkness that conceals the Divine light of the soul. The problem arises in the ego and its shadows, veiling the light of the sacred spirit within us thereby causing distraction. The ruh or soul is ever-perfect, but it can only act through the ego-self in the human state. This causes distractions, errors, regrets, denials and suffering. Yet every individual and every society carry within them the capacity for perfection and destruction."

He takes my hand and with a piercing gaze he says, "If you act as a soul your action will be sublime, if you act as a human, then it may be good or bad, right or wrong. All of these nuances are within existence."

"Shaykhna (Our Shaykh)," I respond, "I understand what you are saying in the realm of meaning, but what about our personal predicament and agony? Why did the Arabs of Palestine find themselves in this miserable situation?"

Shaykh Jamal continued. "If you look at the history of small nations around the world you will find that there were injustices and wrongdoings in every period. Two hundred years ago most of the Middle East was under the loose governance of the Turkish Sultanate. With the decay of that system small nation states began to emerge. The educated thinkers of these lands learnt to acquire nationalistic ideas of identity, mostly imported from Europe. Previously a thin veneer of religion covered up ethnic, racial and other differences, but with the onset of modernity, geographical, cultural and other differences had to be addressed. Conventional Islam was no longer fully alive or compatible with Western influences and education. We have forgotten the importance of social life, kindness, generosity and respect for humanity. We have remained prisoners of the old ways of blind obedience to authority, lacking expression of differences and individuality. By denying outer differences we have lost the path of experiencing inner unity, because differences in views and ideas are often interpreted as dissent and deviation from the norm.

"These are the basic human situations that brought about the Palestinian conflict, which was brought to a head by the persecution of Jews in Europe and the Zionist plan to establish a haven for all Jews, who wanted to reclaim their honour, to feel safe and to control their own destiny. The Arabs also started to formulate some ideas of unity, but they fell into the trap of comparing numbers, not taking into account the advent of new technology and education. Human pride and arrogance blinded them from evaluating the imbalance between their numerical advantage and the benefits of Western education enjoyed by the Jewish immigrants, with the single objective of establishing their state. There are similar tragedies in Asia, Eastern Europe and South America. Religion is often an emotional issue and cause for dissension. This is one of the greatest of human travesties, since the purpose of a true faith is to unify, not to create further dispersion. It is human nature to look for differences, which is a defence mechanism to safeguard life.

"Over decades Arab countries, like Egypt, Iraq, Libya, Morocco, Tunisia, tortuously developed into weak nation states. Certainly there were attempts to implement systems of justice and equity for their citizens. However, there had been centuries of despotism and abusive rulers who had used religion to legitimise their control, so injustices continued to be perpetrated under flimsy veils and political slogans. The energy hungry West cared mostly for short term stability as their needs for oil escalated, thus supporting local rulers, who were often despotic and cruel.

"Nowadays we hear a lot about boat people, the refugees, who are stranded in different locations in the Mediterranean, Indonesia or elsewhere. The Palestinians are another boat people confined in a tight space. Imagine Gaza as a confinement under siege.

"In truth, we are all boat people. Every human being can be regarded as one of the boat people. Your personal canoe is your body, mind and heart, while your family and clan is another boat. We are on a journey from birth to death, both individually and collectively. The human impulse is to survive, to have a measure of equal opportunity and to grow in hope and well-being. This is the underlying drive of every person. We pray that tomorrow will be better than today.

"The aspect of human aspiration that causes discord and confusion arises when people desire happiness that is dependent on outer conditions. The world is based on uncertainty and change, so a state of perpetual happiness can never be attained. Religions have tried to reconcile the spiritual state of peace, contentment and joy with human conditioning, which relates to body, mind and survival. But unless peace, contentment and joy is experienced individually, we will never understand our true destiny. "The dreadful political, economic and human injustices that have been perpetrated on the Palestinian people need to be recognized and addressed. The Qur'an reveals that God does not punish a people, but it is through their own deeds that they bring misery upon themselves. Both Palestinians and Israelis must change their outlook if there is to be any lasting peace and harmony. The Palestinians, Israelis and the Christians all believe that they have some exclusive claim to the soil of a land for historical and religious reasons. Excessive attachment to the things of this world will always cause problems. The lament of the Jews after their exile from the sacred land of their forefathers was beautifully expressed by the medieval Spanish poet Haveli, who made a pilgrimage to Jerusalem.

> And who shall grant me,
> On the wings of eagles,
> To rise and seek thee through the years,
> Until I mingle with thy dust beloved,
> The waters of my tears?
> Shall I not to thy very stones be tender?
> Shall I not kiss them verily?
> Shall not thine earth upon my lips taste sweeter
> Than honey unto me?

"Until there is a true understanding that the outer differences of race, religion, culture and wealth are only veils that conceal our inner sameness, there will be no lasting progress."

There was a knock on the door and a woman in her late twenties entered the room. She was carrying a plate of kebabs, pitta bread and humus. Shaykh Jamal introduces her as his daughter Asiya, a lecturer in anthropology at the Hebrew University of Jerusalem. "We will ask Asiya," he says "about the future of our country."

Asiya is eager to expound on the mess that past generations on both sides had made. She thinks change will come because of increased involvement from both Palestinian and Israeli women.

"Women," she says with a smile, "are always more practical and compassionate in their approach. Mothers on both sides want security for their families and an end to conflict. There are many Jews, both in Israel and outside, who are only too aware of the injustices that have been done to the Palestinians. I have some Jewish friends at university and we often discuss what can be done to bring about reconciliation between our peoples. There is an organisation called Parent Circle Family Forum set up by people who have experienced personal trauma in their own lives and want to bring about a better understanding between our two peoples. They send speakers to universities. Last month I went to one of these talks. There was a Palestinian woman whose husband had been killed by an Israeli soldier. It was a dreadful mistake; the soldier had thought he was armed and fired. She was on the podium with an Israeli mother whose only son had been killed in Gaza. Instead of becoming angry and bitter they travel around the country together, giving talks to inspire people to discover the common humanity that binds us all.

"Last week a Jewish girl from New York came to see me to discuss what could be done to help the Bedouin women and children in the desert areas. Esther is studying at the university here and had been moved by the conditions in the settlements. She wanted my advice regarding what she and other American Jews could do to help. An organisation called the Jewish National Fund collects funds from international Jewry for projects within Israel. Esther had been aware of its contribution to ecological issues for years. What could be more meritorious than planting trees? However, when she saw some of those trees being planted on Palestinian owned properties in the South without the owner's permission, Esther realised this was closer to green washing than philanthropy. People of conscience like Esther are living proof of the saying, the antidote to any poison lies near its source. As for our Muslim brothers in other countries, they do give us aid, but never enough to make sufficient impact on our suffering. Instead we have become a symbol of Western injustice."

I interrupt Asiya to ask her, as an anthropologist, what she thinks the future holds for the Abrahamic faiths. She replies, "I think the world is starting to shed years of religious, racial and ethnic identities. It is now science that will show us the direction to experience unity. We are entering a new era where every person needs to experience God's light within their own heart directly. My husband, Ahmed, believes that organized religion has had its advantages, but is now failing. That does not mean that people are abandoning their spiritual quests."

Eager to hear his opinions, I ask her where I can find Ahmed. She hands me a card with the address of Café One. "Ahmed is always there," she says, "and he will welcome you." She leaves the room and Shaykh Jamal turns to me with a reassuring smile. "Times have changed," he says, "in one way it seems that we are further away from what we consider to be our deen (religion, life transaction). In another way we know that God is the ultimate victor and He is supreme at all times. Everyone is seeking the truth more desperately nowadays, but on a personal and individual basis, rather than a collective one. Some of us began to worship our religion instead of God and that distraction is a universal sickness that accompanies organised religion. If you spend some time with Ahmed, you may realise that despite your dissatisfaction with what you see around you, there is hope on the horizon."

When I arrive at the café, Ahmed, a pleasant looking man in his thirties gives me a warm welcome and leads me to his private office. I ask him what his father-in-law meant when he said that the present may be gloomy, but the future is much better. "He is talking about me," Ahmed replies. "I had become very disillusioned with my religion and the only thing that saved me were the verses of the Qur'an about how Allah never wrongs a people, instead they wrong themselves, and how people follow the habits of their predecessors. Interpretations of these verses can often be misleading and far from the original message. When I met Shaykh Jamal he reassured me that I had been spared the lifeless religion that I inherited and that my love of truth would guide me. He gave me selective verses of Qur'an to recite, memorize and live by. These verses have transformed me and made me realise that truth is universal and encompasses everything in life, including what we consider as falsehood. Darkness exists because there is light and it is goodness that shows us what is evil. It is best to look at every vice or wrong-doing and turn away from it to face the virtue or the light that illumines all.

"The wrong-doing of the ultra-nationalist Zionists is simply a repetition of what they had suffered. I don't condone it, but I have compassion for them and I know that after a few generations they will realize that the impoverished and persecuted Palestinians are, in essence, the same as them."

As I headed back to my hotel, Ahmed's last words echoed in my mind.

"All of humanity are groping for the heavens. We all want to experience the elusive perfection of Jerusalem on earth. If I don't discover that light in my own heart I will be accusing everyone else of wrong-doing. Human life on earth is a work in progress and God is eternally patient."

36
Tajiki Snake Venom

After the fall of the Soviet Union, Russia slowly began to open to tourists. Always suffering from wanderlust, I made plans with a friend to visit Uzbekistan. That is where I met the formidable Mrs Shaheedi from the small neighbouring country, Tajikistan.

I heard of her from a man who attended one of my lectures in London. He had heard about my plans to visit Uzbekistan and arranged for me to meet with Mrs Shaheedi. He told me that she was the daughter of the most famous trading family in Tajikistan. She was therefore well connected, very hospitable and she would be able to advise us and help us in this foreign country. She had also read some of my books and would be pleased to meet me in person.

We flew to Tashkent, the capital of Uzbekistan, and booked into an enormous hotel that was very clumsily designed to look like an open book. There must have been more than a thousand rooms. Every floor had its own concierges and ours were two frightening hefty ladies who had made it clear that no nonsense would be tolerated on their floor. Tired from the flight, my companion and I disappeared into our rooms for a good night's sleep, only to be woken around midnight by a big fuss in the corridor. It was Mrs Shaheedi quarrelling with the scary ladies, insisting she wanted to meet us that very minute.

Still heavy with sleep, we were introduced and after refreshments were ordered, she explained the urgency of her visit. She knew we were only going to be in the city for a day or two and didn't want to miss us. She had been traveling and when she arrived in Pakistan, she heard I was already in Uzbekistan. She wanted to come and see us before we proceeded with our journey, but there were no flights for a few days. Then she heard that a cargo flight would leave that day to Tashkent carrying some donations from the Pakistani government to Uzbekistan. True to her formidable nature, she contacted the president and asked to be put on the cargo plane.

We became good friends and kept in touch regularly. Two or three years after my visit to Uzbekistan, I had to go to Gothenburg to give lectures at a Sufi conference. Mrs Shaheedi decided to attend the conference with her niece and nephew. Her niece was a very talented violinist who had hopes of studying music in Sweden, while her nephew was a gifted young man who had his sights on a British university. Sweden was to be the springboard for their careers. But their journey to Sweden is quite an amazing story.

To travel abroad from Tajikistan, you first had to fly to Moscow with plenty of rubles, buy a ticket to your destination there, and then continue your journey. So, with stacks of rubles in Mrs Shaheedi's bag, the three of them went to the airport in Dushanbe. A few friends and relatives were at the airport to see them off. Among them was a young teacher from a local agricultural school. He had a small red velvet bag in his hand, the type that closed with a drawstring, and gave it to Mrs Shaheedi. In the bag was a vial containing the venom of a rare Tajiki snake. He was a collector of snake venom, but he said that nobody there had any interest in it. He was hoping she could sell it abroad and that they could share the money. Then the call for boarding came. Mrs Shaheedi didn't really know how to respond, but she thanked the man and dropped the vial into her handbag.

While they were on the plane to Moscow, the unthinkable happened – the captain made an announcement that the ruble had collapsed. Whatever it had been worth an hour ago, it was now less than ten percent of that. Mrs Shaheedi never thought for a moment that the thousands of rubles she had secured for their trip to Sweden would not even pay for one air ticket. Fortunately, she managed to borrow some money from relatives in Moscow, got the tickets, and the party of three was on their way again.

One of the men in the group of people attending my lectures happened to be an industrial chemist. Mrs Shaheedi told him about the vial of venom and he was immediately interested. He was sure it was very valuable, and that it could be used to develop an anti-venom. He was right; a pharmaceutical firm actually bought it for a few thousand dollars. So it happened that Tajiki snake venom paid for Mrs Shaheedi's visit. The same venom made it possible to stay long enough to find a scholarship for her niece to study music and for her nephew to get into one of the best universities in Britain.

Some people might say that it was just a fortunate coincidence. Others might say that it is good to be reminded every now and then of how the unseen can sometimes shape what we consider to be a tangible world and that it is up to us to read the signs correctly.

37
Walking on Water

The weekend long international conference on the rise of global spirituality was coming to an end. During the break I went outside with my cup of coffee and found a bench at the edge of a picturesque pond, looking forward to a little quiet time by myself. Just as I sat down a young man who had greeted me earlier that morning approached me. Ivan politely asked permission to join me. I couldn't refuse his courteous request.

He mentioned how my story regarding the danger of mimicking a teacher or a master had struck him. I had emphasized the risk of imbibing the higher consciousness of an enlightened being and assuming that you now have constant access to this state. I had been trying to demonstrate how there were many pitfalls on the ladder to higher consciousness.

Ivan told me how he had fallen into that trap after several years of being close to his guru. He said that he had become like the moon reflecting the light of the sun. When he got married he assumed the role of being the teacher, and as a result the relationship crumbled after only a few months. With a sad smile he confessed that he now realised how he had deceived himself. He had to acknowledge that he had suffered from numerous delusions, like being liberated from his ego; thinking that his lower self was dead; that he was wise and godly; that he was special in God's eyes; that misery is caused by people's own faults; that he was a soldier of truth and reality, and that he was following in the footsteps of the great masters and prophets.

My coffee was finished and it was time to leave. I turned to him and said, "All of these pitfalls and distractions are part of our journey towards higher consciousness. Jesus called one of his disciples to follow him as he walked on water. The fellow obviously had a great deal of self-doubt, but upon Jesus's insistence to walk towards him, he forgot himself for a moment. When he reached the master the thought came to him that he was now as great as Jesus. At that point, he began to sink.

"It is not unusual to fall into this trap. Our life is based on the rational mind and habits, but as we begin to experience the higher domains of spiritual realities, we also run the risk of falling back. A skier at the learning slopes is safer when he falls than the one who is higher up the mountain. The dangers are always more serious near the peak.

"Bear in mind that there are basically two spheres of consciousness. The first one is conditioned by culture, genes and the environment, which aids our physical and emotional growth. This culminates in the acquisition of earthly skills and knowledge. Wisdom in this zone is rational and follows the laws of reason and causality. The other zone encompasses everything in existence and has its own subtle laws and patterns. The risk for any seeker of spiritual liberation is mixing up the two realms. It is the in-between state that most seekers suffer from. It takes a lot of practice, reflection and good fortune."

Ivan seemed even more confused than when he first approached me. We shook hands and I encouraged him to have faith, trust and willingness to face occasional failures and disappointments. I reminded him that as long as we live, our ego will be alive. We should just keep our focus on the eternal light and occasionally we will catch glimpses of it from within our own heart. It is only by grace that we transcend the ego-self and fly towards cosmic consciousness.

38
The Shaykh of the Buffalo

I adored Sufi Barkat Ali. He was one of the greatest, most respected and most generous Sufis of the twentieth century, and I cherish the pleasure and privilege of having visited him several times. He was always surrounded by dozens of poor peasants, well-dressed young people and women with special requests. Most notable, however, were the solemn, long bearded and tunic clad Sufi types who had an air about of them of being the only true followers of the Shaykh.

As a young man he had served in the Indian army while India was still under the rule of the British Crown. His family and friends had expected a bright future for him, but his British superiors soon realized that he had no ambition to flourish as a soldier. "They dismissed me for being too God-intoxicated," he told me with a mischievous smile. "Can you believe that? To be mad about God is the only true sanity!"

After his dismissal he immigrated to Pakistan and settled in the Punjab province where he established the Dar al-Ehsan centre for orphans, refugees and other seekers to be housed and educated. At the time Sufism had started to become popular in America and Europe and the Shaykh also welcomed Western Sufis. For a few months every year the centre became a hub of activity when the annual eye-camp was set up and doctors from around the country came to treat cataracts and other eye ailments free of charge.

Apart from his teaching and community service, Sufi Barkat Ali also started a project to find and repair copies of the Qur'an. One of his followers had set up a collection point outside Lahore and every few days a small lorry load of jumbled manuscripts arrived at the centre. It was quite a sight to see the hundreds of orphans sifting through these manuscripts. The torn pages and parts of the Qur'an would be lovingly matched and patched by the adult students to produce complete copies of the Qur'an. Within a few years large halls were filled up with every imaginable size and age of manuscript, some even handwritten. I was shown a Qur'an the size of a thumb and another one measuring perhaps three by three metres. It took three people to turn the pages to prevent them from tearing.

Sufi Barkat Ali suffered many setbacks in his life, especially with his own family, but his sense of humor was never affected by it. He was always the jester, highlighting the lighter side of any situation. One thing he enjoyed was afternoon strolls in the mango orchards with his prayer bead carriers in tow. The string was about five meters long and had to be carried by eager young followers who competed for this honour daily. One might think this to be a quiet meditative activity, but every so often shrieks and screams would echo from the orchards, because the Shaykh had started weaving through the trees in a random manner, twirling and tanging the beads, causing absolute consternation among the hapless bead carriers.

I once asked a friend from Faisalabad, a local university professor, to fill a large container with food items, like ghee, rice, chickpeas, a tea chest and a sack of flour and deliver it to the camp. The next day I heard that instead of flour, a large bunch of cut flowers, more specifically, roses, had been delivered. To be fair, this was probably an honest mistake since it had been well-known that the Shaykh used rose petals as remedies for different ailments. But the spirited Sufi Barkat Ali did not let this mistake go without getting a little merriment out of it. He called his helpers, instructed the visitors to take up position in his prayer niche and started pelting them with the flowers.

There is one particular day that I would never forget. As always, Sufi Barkat Ali was surrounded by a large group of admirers and followers. By that time the calling to teach had already chosen me, and I was visiting in the capacity of a Sufi master. I was still somewhat unsure of what the best way would be to reach people. I quite liked the idea of settling in a rural area like the Shaykh and letting people come to me. As if reading my mind, he suddenly pointed at me, a smile on his face so big I could see the space where one front tooth was missing, and he proclaimed, "If anyone here wants to learn the science of divine Oneness, you should follow him! As for myself, you have already witnessed it several times, the villagers come to me to pray for their buffalo to bear more than one baby, so I am the Shaykh for the buffalo! But you," he said, both arms outstretched in my direction, "you should roam the world! You do not belong to any specific place, so reconcile yourself with being in exile fulltime."

As a parting gift, he gave me eight beautifully bound handwritten Qur'ans. "These are for the eight Sufi centres you will establish around the world," he said. And the rest, as the saying goes, is history.

39
Silent Retreat

Nothing benefits the heart more than a spiritual seclusion, whereby it enters the domain of true reflections.

Ibn 'Ata'Alah

Christopher was approaching forty. The routine of his life in England seemed mundane and bleak and the pursuit of material success did not bring any lasting fulfilment.

He slept badly and one morning, while it was still dark outside, he got up. While he waited for his tea to brew, he remembered a conversation he had had with his grandmother before she passed away. She had told him that silence was the gateway to knowledge that encompasses all other knowledge. At the time he didn't pay much attention to it, but now he felt the need to find out what she had meant by it.

One of his friends had recently returned from a trip to Morocco and had met Sidi Karim where he resided just outside Tétouan. Sidi Karim was known as one of three living saints. Christopher decided to go to Morocco to meet the Saint. Maybe it would help to find a way out of his growing feelings of futility.

Tétouan was a charming city with a rich history. When the Muslims and Jews were expelled from Grenada in the 15th century, they settled in Tétouan and tried to rebuild a town like they had been used to, using similar building material, architectural styles, techniques and colours. Nowadays the orchards outside the city had become popular with tourists. At one particular fig orchard you would find Sidi Karim, sitting at the door of his hut most of the time, reciting the Qur'an. Sometimes he would take a break and talk to the curious tourists. Christopher prayed that he would be able to meet him and have a chance to talk to him.

His prayers were answered. Sidi Karim gazed into Christopher's eyes and said, "You need to empty yourself of yourself. Let go of the illusions of who you are, which were acquired in the pursuit of survival and within conditioned consciousness. To find lasting meaning, one must purify the mind from the belief of separation from the mysterious reality, called spirit or divine soul. It is the illusion of separation that brings about anxiety. You have to learn how to stop time."

"Forgive me, Shaykh," Christopher replied, "but I don't know how to do that."

The Shaykh, recognizing the sincerity and desperation of his quest, offered a solution — a silent retreat. Excitement surged through Christopher as he envisioned a serene cave tucked away in the mountain, or a cabin in the forest where he could immerse himself in silence. He was to return in three days to start his retreat.

However, reality diverged rudely from his dreams when, three days later, Sidi Karim led him to a small room adjacent to his humble house. The space was dimly lit, with basic amenities and the constant bustle of workers on the farm outside. There was very little silence. The Shaykh, sensing Christopher's disillusionment, calmly instructed him, "No talking, no reading, no writing, and no recitation. Just embrace the emptiness within. It will be difficult at first to find that complete silence within, but it will get easier. Be in the moment, lose everything that is distracting you from the immensity of timelessness, which gives birth to infinite strings of now – now – now. And when your mind starts to wander, contemplate your mortality."

For three days Christopher was alone. Initially he struggled with the external noise and the absence of the picturesque retreat he had envisioned. Yet, within the confines of the simple room, he began to discover the elusive silence he had sought. He learned to confront the illusions that had clouded his existence. The ceaseless pursuit of joy and security melted away. Embracing the simplicity of his surroundings, he found that silence wasn't just an absence of noise, but a state of emptiness within.

On the last evening he had a vision of his own funeral. He saw young men carrying his body. There were several people close by, sombre but not grieving. He cried so much that his clothes were drenched with his tears. Beholding the end of his biographical existence was extremely liberating because it was witnessed by his own perfect, eternal soul.

In that small, dank room, Christopher had discovered the profound truth imparted by Sidi Karim — the path to meaning lies not in the external, but in the silent depths of one's own soul.

40

The Wali of the Atlas Mountains

Sidi Mustafa was regarded by many Sufis to be an enlightened being. He lived in a small village in the middle of the Atlas Mountains.

When I first met him, he was in his eighties and almost completely blind. He lived in a small house where his elder daughter was looking after him. For forty years he had served teachers, masters and Shaykhs, but never claimed to have any special merits or powers, although many learned people acknowledged him as a wali – a friend of God.

The house, perched on a rock right next to a fast stream coming down from the forest, had three floors. At the entrance, leading into the kitchen, there was a small cage with a noisy chicken, which I later learnt would give one egg every day. A blue door opened to a long reception room with a low level banquette all around, where the Wali would spend most of his days. The room could accommodate two dozen people and had two high windows with a magnificent view of the stream of water flowing down from the mountain. On both sides of the stream mulberry trees were interspersed with cork trees, which continued into the forests. Upstairs there were two small bedrooms and the second story had a small flat roof with one water tap next to a bucket.

People who knew the Wali for many years confirmed that he had been fasting ever since they had known him. He would only have one simple meal in the evening. On the first day of my visit I asked him about his fasting and he said he just followed what his body told him. He told me, as a young man, he had worked in the forest cutting timber, which was physically very demanding. During the time that he was involved in building a zawiya (a Sufi centre) on the edge of the desert for a Tijani Shaykh, his concern about earthly life had almost vanished and was replaced with the delights of the constant light, which pervades the outer and inner worlds. He said that by the time he was thirty he would neglect his body's needs for long periods of time, until an outer event would remind him of it. Once he had secluded himself in the mountain and after three days of no food or drink, he was very weak and started praying for relief. He fell asleep and was awakened by a dog sniffing him. The dog's owner soon followed; he was a hunter and insisted on sharing his food with the Wali. They feasted on a rabbit he had caught and drank sweet almond milk. This experience taught him that he should not be concerned with physical needs; it will always be provided if his concern remained at the altar of the Provider. The next day he dreamt that God spoke to him and said that once you have done your best in the visible world, you can trust fully in the invisible, for everything emanates from the unseen.

The Wali asked me to return the next morning. When I arrived, a dozen European converts had filled the room in great anticipation, looking around for clues of spiritual insights. The group leader asked the Wali questions regarding the discovery of truth and being with God. Meanwhile, his daughter came in to serve sweet Moroccan tea and the room fell into anticipative silence. Then the Wali's bright face beamed as he told the visitors to stop wasting energy and to stick to the ultimate truth, that there is none other than the One.

The leader of the group offered the Wali several parcels and gifts, including some Moroccan money. At this point the Wali turned to a man sitting to his right and asked him how much money he had. "Three-hundred dollars and some dinars," the man replied. The Wali asked, "What about the two-hundred-and-sixty pounds in the other pocket of your jacket?" The man blushed, took out the money and presented it to the Wali, who promptly gave it back and told him he should keep it, because he would need it the next day, when his car would break down.

He warned another visitor that his good opinion of himself was his biggest stumbling block in spiritual progress. This man was respected amongst the British converts and the Wali was concerned that this identity could prevent him from realizing the perfect beauty and prevalence of sacred reality. He warned against the snugness of the newly discovered religion and the illusion of being special.

When everyone left, we sat quietly, enjoying the view through the window. Now and then the Wali whispered to himself, wrapped up in his own world. We started talking about miracles. His opinion was that all existence and whatever appears or does not, are all facets of the sacred miracle. Whichever thread of reality you handle, you are tagging on this original Oneness. He put his arm around me and said anything that appears indicates its origin, which is unseen; trust in all and realize the original light in your own heart.

His voice suddenly changed to a serious tone. "Do not trust my daughter who looks after me," he said. I asked if is she was the one with a baby strapped to her back. "Yes," he replied, "she has much anxiety about provisions and now she asks for money from my visitors. Hopefully once her child grows up she will become more aware and trust the real Provider. The child depends on the parent, the adults depend on their own ability, but the sage depends on the One from whom all emanates."

41
Distorted Similarity

Rajab started his journey on the Sufi path by buying a few books, which he enjoyed reading every day. Some of his habits changed straightaway. He began getting up before dawn each day, admiring the sunrise and then reading and making notes from his new books. When his Sufi uncle heard about this, he advised Rajab to find a good teacher, adding, "It is only by living the teaching that the Divine will prevail over the human will." Rajab had heard the Chishtis talk about being at the gate of Jannah, the paradise awaiting those who could stay on the righteous path, and that this experience could be achieved by dying into your shaykh, to make your will subservient to his. So that is what he set out to do.

> *We are impressionable creatures and need outer references until we access our own inner soul – the resident teacher.*

When Rajab first met his Shaykh, he felt awkward and self-conscious. After several meetings he understood that the ego-self veil was the barrier to the inner soul. He gradually learnt to transcend the self. It wasn't easy to give up his self-image, worries about daily necessities and other worldly concerns and desires. To move from self-concern to soul-awareness turned out to be much more difficult than he had imagined. After a few years a bond of unconditional trust developed between master and disciple and Rajab ended up following his Shaykh's instructions diligently and without question.

After some years with his Shaykh, Rajab began to feel lonely and in need of a house partner. He was ready to get married, but how to choose the right woman? Since it was the Chishti tradition to live like your master and to follow in his footsteps, he decided to look for a wife like the one his Shaykh had, even though she was considered to be the most difficult woman in town. She was impossible to please, always rude and demanding. People avoided her with fervor.

It didn't take Rajab long to find a suitable bride. She had a reputation for bad manners and a quick temper. But within a few weeks after they had gotten married, he realized his terrible situation. Day after day his wife's conduct became more unbearable. Her demands, complaints and constant shouting at Rajab brought him down to his knees. It had become almost impossible for him to cope with his duties as a spiritual leader. Exhausted and disheartened, he decided to visit his Shaykh and plead for his advice.

After presenting his impossible situation with much sighing, frantic gesticulation and long pauses, Rajab was dumbfounded when the Shaykh broke into a fit of laughter. When he eventually stopped laughing, he beckoned for Rajab to come closer and put his hand on him reassuringly. With an amused look on his face, he asked, "Is the diet of a baby the same as that of a child? And is the diet of a child the same as that of an old man? What is poison for you, might be medicine for me. You may follow your Shaykh up to a point, but you should not blindly mimic him!"

42
Failed Departure

Nigel opened his eyes with difficulty and stared at the fluorescent tube on the ceiling. He felt extremely drowsy. "Thank God, you're awake." It was his mother's voice. He looked at her, confused about why she was there. And then he remembered. He had taken a handful of sleeping pills and hoped to never wake up again. Silent tears pooled in his eyes. He realized that he was in hospital and was devastated to still be alive.

He had been so tired of life that he could not see the point of continuing with what appeared to be a futile exercise. For many months he had contemplated ending his life, and the night before he decided it was now or never.

Nigel had always been a serious boy. His father had died when he was only ten. Angela, his mother turned their home into a guest house to support the two of them. Nigel never had a close relationship with his father and therefore didn't really miss him. As a child he preferred to spend time alone with his computer and books. He adored his mother, and was proud of her for taking such good care of them.

"Sweetheart, do you need anything?" Angela asked. He looked at her and felt a pang of guilt. "How …?" he asked. "I just had a feeling I should phone you last night. And when you didn't answer, I was worried, so I rushed to your apartment and let myself in with the key you gave me, and …" She grabbed both his hands and started crying.

During his teenage years the nerdy youngster would often stare endlessly into the night sky, see the myriads of stars and feel a sense of his own insignificance. He became overwhelmed by the impermanence of everything that existed on earth.

Throughout his university years Nigel became increasingly haunted by his sense of purposelessness. For a while the discovery of girls, weed and the university party scene dulled the search for meaning. After graduation he took a job, rather reluctantly, with a firm of management consultants. It was a concession to his mother, who found his musings incomprehensible. She attended church weekly, believed in a kindly God and some sort of life after death. Nigel was the main worry in her existence. She couldn't understand why her son didn't just desire the normal things in life: a good job, a nice house and a family.

Nigel did try. He started dating Jane, one of his colleagues. She was a wonderful girl and he enjoyed their thought-provoking conversations. But when Jane started looking at engagement rings and houses, he felt let down and he ended the relationship.

Social life had lost its attraction and Nigel became a recluse. He even avoided his mother, because he knew how disappointed she was. Then, one of Nigel's university friends killed himself. In the note he had left, he apologized to his family for the hurt his death would cause. He explained how he had struggled with depression for years and that he just couldn't find meaning or purpose in his life. Therefore he had decided to merely bring forward the date of his inevitable demise. A few months after Edward's sudden death, Nigel resigned from his job and started planning his own exit from this meaningless life. Only, he did not succeed.

Nigel had been transferred to the psychiatric ward. He had spent hours with a therapist and after a few weeks he was discharged. As soon as he got home, he flushed all the pills he had been prescribed down the drain.

One morning, feeling wretched after having suffered from flu, he decided that some fresh air might do him good. He ventured out to an organic market where he found a herbal remedies stand manned by a fellow in late middle age, wrinkled and bronzed, clearly spending much of his life in the outdoors. He sported a neat beard, but his most distinguishing feature was a pair of piercing blue eyes. They started talking and Nigel learnt that Jim grew the organic herbs from which he made his tinctures himself. He suggested an anti-bacterial anti-viral combination and as he handed it to Nigel, he said, "The flu isn't your biggest problem, is it?" The question took Nigel by surprise and he started rattling out all the unanswered questions that had been troubling him for years.

Jim listened patiently. He asked Nigel if he would like to talk more after closing time. Nigel accepted the invitation. He was baffled by how vocal he had been with this complete stranger. When he saw people started packing up, he made his way back to Jim and helped him pack up the stand.

A short while later they were sipping coffee at a nearby café. They were chatting away, as if Jim and he were old friends. Nigel said, "Everyone seems to be occupied with achieving material success, and I am always conscious that all of these endeavours will end and inevitably people will fall back into despair and inertia. I cannot see the point of making an effort if the whole thing eventually returns back to nothingness." Jim looked at him quizzically and replied, "You have a very negative outlook on life. Who, may I ask, were the philosophers or spiritual masters, who have influenced you?" "Schopenhauer and Camus," confessed Nigel, "and neither of them gave me any plausible reason to have personal drive and ambition in this life, nor any hope for the future." Jim took a few seconds before responding. "Your problem seems to be that you are completely wrapped up in yourself. As long as you have minimal healthy interaction with the world around you, the depression and sense of futility will persist. Would you consider coming to stay with me for a while? I think it might help you to get a more rounded perspective on life. Have you ever read Voltaire's 'Candide'?" Nigel admitted that he had not. "Well," Jim continued, "he ends the novel with the conclusion that cultivating one's garden is the key to happiness. It is interesting that, apart from meaning to farm, the French word 'cultiver' also has the connotation of improving yourself." Nigel didn't really understand the metaphor and said as much. "The garden refers to your own life, of course," Jim explained, "but a garden is small. So what Voltaire meant was that one should not be too concerned about changing the world or other people's problems. Tend your own garden and find joy in the simple pleasures of life. And while Voltaire meant this in the metaphorical sense, I have an actual garden that needs constant attention." Nigel smiled for the first time in months and agreed to help Jim with his garden.

Jim worked him so hard the first few days he regretted agreeing to this version of slave labour. But slowly a new rhythm slipped into place. At the end of each day Nigel could see the results of his labours in the herb garden. He began to feel a sense of achievement and connection with the earth. He was learning from Jim about the properties of the various medicinal herbs and in the evenings they would prepare tinctures from the fresh plants they had gathered. For the first time in his life Nigel felt really useful. And in Jim he found a wise and compassionate mentor.

One evening Jim asked him if he had ever experienced the vast expanse of no-thingness. Nigel had taken a cursory glance at Buddhist and Hindu teachings, so he was aware of the concept, but he said that he had not had any deep personal experience. Jim explained that all religious and spiritual paths profess that life emerges from a vast infinite zone and returns back to it. "The purpose in life is to experience and realize this truth, which is not confined to space or time," he said. "Enlightened people and prophets describe this state as bliss. What we describe as happiness is merely a by-product of a state that is beyond that of mind or thought. So, if I can give you a prescription for your life, it is to practice and realize that state within you. As for the outside world and the need for a career and interaction with others, these are all necessary but secondary issues. As you have always intuitively felt, worldly success or harmonious relationships are all transient. They can only bring a superficial level of happiness or contentment."

"But why isn't the light inside us obvious from the beginning?" Nigel exclaimed. "That would certainly have made my life a lot easier! Can you please show me how to get to this light?" Ignoring Nigel's exasperation, Jim answered him softly, "No person, no matter how enlightened they are, can give you that light. They can only mirror it. That light shines even in darkness, but your human status veils it from you. The seed of a plant contains within it the secret of a beautiful flower or fruit. The outer shell that protects the seed must wither away for germination and growth to take place. So, too, must our outer delusions and ego vanish before the inner truth appears."

"You and your metaphors," Nigel said affectionately.

"I think you are ready to leave here," said Jim. "You need to go and hug your mother and promise her that you will never attempt to snuff out your own light again. And then you have to start tending your own garden."

43
Laylah al Ahmad

Laylah was sitting cross-legged on her patio swing high up on the seventh floor of her Beirut apartment. She was staring into the distance while gently rocking the swing. In her lap was a bundle of crumpled tissues and on her cheeks the evidence of many tears.

It was the day that her divorce had been finalized and apart from feeling heartbroken, she felt lost and very unsure of her future. Being born into a prominent, powerful family and having had the best education in France apparently did not safeguard one against a disrupted life.

She had fallen in love with Iskandar ten years ago and although he had the reputation of a religious firebrand, she married him, albeit against her family's wishes. She supported him for years while he was spreading his message of Shia revival. They had decided not to have children so that he could pursue his dangerous work. Well, it would be more correct to say that Iskandar had decided it would be best for them not to have children and Laylah went along with it. Who was she to stand in the way of her husband's revolutionary zeal?

Every few months the couple would spend time with Laylah's family on their farm. These visits began to poison their relationship as her family kept expressing their doubts about Iskandar. After one such a visit, back in their apartment in Beirut, Iskandar asked for a divorce. He said that he had to go on a long term mission somewhere in South America with a possible fatal outcome and did not want her to wonder if he would ever return. Laylah was distraught, but not surprised.

The sun was beginning to set, but Laylah was still swinging, contemplating what she should do next. She went to bed wondering if she would ever get married again. The strong maternal desires that had been plaguing her the last few years would not subside. She fell asleep with an unfinished prayer on her lips. Only a few hours later she woke up with a start and felt a strong inner voice rising within her. Years of doubts and anguish began to bubble up at the same time. She was questioning the meaning and purpose of her experiences. Why had she fallen in love with Iskandar? Why did he have to leave her? Why had this happened to her? She knew that her religion would not be able to answer any of her questions and despondently she stayed in bed until midmorning.

Laylah remained maddeningly restless. She phoned her father, but he was of no help in easing her anguish. Her mother tried to comfort her with words of hope and encouragement, while her younger sister was eager to set her up with a new man. She decided to go out for some exercise and fresh air. Wandering through the streets without paying attention to her surroundings, occasionally bumping into other pedestrians, she finally stopped at a shop that sold old Persian carpets. As she ran her hands over some of the carpets on display, an idea popped into her head – she would visit Aunt Salima, she was an excellent listener and always had the best advice. With a beautiful thickly woven prayer mat under her arm, she already felt better and hurried home to phone her aunt.

Aunt Salima was extremely pleased with the mat and did something unexpected. She invited Laylah to pray with her on the new rug. During the prayer Laylah felt her inner voice calm down and for the first time in years she could feel the source of life in her heart stirring again. After they had prayed, her aunt advised her to go to Mecca for Umra, and then asked her to write down some instructions as to what to do when she got there.

It took a few months to plan the trip, but eventually Laylah found herself sitting close to the Prophet's tomb at Bab Gibril, reciting the words her aunt had given her. Suddenly she fainted and had a vision.

When the mosque guard awakened her, the vision became clear to her in an instant. It was like a blinding light that obliterated her entire past, and all that she could hear was the Prophet's voice saying, "This is what happened to me in the cave. You came to me bereft and helpless, and the least I could do is to let the light of that cave touch you. Now you can get up and start your life afresh. Forget everything except the present. Go, and set up an orphanage in your village in the south and raise a new generation of young ones."

Laylah returned to Beirut eager to educate herself about everything that needed to be done to embark on her new mission. She drew strength from the Prophet and the passion that characterized his life. She was looking forward to love and care for the children at the orphanage. It was what she had always wanted, even though it came to her through a very different path than the one she had imagined.

44
Sadiq, the Martyr

*This life is a preparation and a joyful anticipation
of eternal life to which we all return.*

Sadiq means he who speaks the truth. He often thought of changing his name, because he had realized that most human experiences contain more lies than truth.

Many years ago, Sadiq was tasked with driving me around and protecting me on my visit to Tehran. During our time together he told me his life story and a special bond was formed between us.

He was raised with the sound of Qur'an and the praise of Muhammed. As a descendant of the Prophet, he felt privileged and obligated to honour what he believed in. When he was seventeen years old, he was conscripted into the army to fight the neighboring enemies.

After a few years he had been accepted as an officer into the new army for special duty assignments. As an officer he fought in forty recorded battles over a period of three years, in which an estimated six hundred people were killed.

During the first one his deputy had been shot and Sadiq had to carry him for nearly two days to get back to a place of safety. With almost every battle he had to rescue someone who had been badly injured. With only the tools in his backpack, he buried twenty-nine people, most of whom had been like brothers to him. At twenty-five years of age no-one who started out fighting with him was alive anymore.

After one particularly traumatizing experience he returned home to an overjoyed circle of family and friends. Everybody thought that he had died months before in an air attack on the rebels. It took three days for him to recover from the physical and mental shock. During this time he was either asleep or in a daze. It was his mother's voice and chicken soup that brought him back to reality. On the third day, emerging from a deep sleep, he gazed at her face for several minutes and said that the ray of light from her was beginning to dispel the immense darkness of fear and grief that he was carrying with him. He then told her what had happened to him.

A raid on a government outpost where there were a considerable amount of high-tech equipment and materials had been executed. But it turned out to be a trap orchestrated by one of their own leaders. When the battle was over, nine of their men were dead. He was very troubled and thought that he couldn't live with his name any longer. He felt surrounded by darkness, shadows and veils covering the truth, and his name "Truth-sayer" felt like mockery. His mother's reassurances about accepting God's will didn't appease him. He told his mother that he was not concerned about God's will, rather he wanted an answer to the question of what to do with his own life.

Sadiq confessed that during the forty raids that he had led, death was not uncommon. Initially, he would go into shock or fear. But after a while he learnt to stop his mind and lose all sense of time and place. When he came around again, injured and dragging himself out of the battle, it would take him a while to reconcile with his earthly consciousness again. As time went on, he became used to this way of life; constantly touching death whilst experiencing a more sublime level of life. Eventually he was allowed to retire with full honours.

I assured him that the numerous raids he had been through and his constant closeness to death was the best preparation to experience the presence of eternal life within his heart. I explained to him that every time he had been injured or escaped death in a battle, his inner light became stronger, giving him access to the zone of the sacred life within him.

He turned to me thoughtfully and said, "It must be this quality that has attracted you to me. Many people like me and want my company, but very few know it is because most of the time I am not propelled by my mind or thoughts. Switching off my mind became the easiest part of my life. My eyes and ears pick up the signals, but I have no response. Maybe only five people in this world understand me and what had happened to me, and you are one of them. I know that I do not belong here, and yet I am still on this earth. My mind is only a tiny fraction of the world I am in. I am aware of the transience of life, which is only a prelude to completeness after death."

Sadiq finally found the answer as to what to do with his life. He used the generous salary he received after leaving the army to build a cemetery in the desert and he also lived there, waiting for his turn to leave the earthly life behind. It was mostly young martyrs who were laid to rest there and Sadiq also used it as a place to celebrate the purpose of life and the journey hereafter. He wanted people to celebrate the victory of the soul and eternal life, not grieving over the loss of a body. People would go there with drums and flags, singing praises to God.

Sometimes Sadiq would feel as if the clothes were being pulled from his body by those who went before him. He could hear their voices telling him, 'It is better here than where we were'. Other times the hushed voices asked him when he would be joining them.

Sadiq made peace with his name when he understood the ultimate truth – the human soul belongs to paradise forever and the experience of earthly transition is only a preparation to leave cheerfully.

45
Liberating Education

In the years before Grace had started working at the church, she often considered her life a complete failure. She grew up at the small Swedish missionary compound in the Valley of a Thousand Hills in Kwa-Zulu Natal. Her mother worked at the compound and always took her beautiful intelligent daughter along and eventually Grace ended up working in the canteen at the school.

At sixteen her life changed irrevocably: she had fallen pregnant and one of the priests was suspended…

Years later, working in Cape Town, Grace got caught up in the drug trafficking business, mainly because she didn't have money for her daughter's education. The drug bosses had taken their toll on her to the point that she stopped caring for herself. All her passion had been focused on her daughter; she was adamant that she should have an education and earn a professional degree.

Grace looked much older than her age when her daughter finally received a degree in accounting and business administration from the University of Cape Town. A proud mother photographed with her daughter in her graduation cap and gown. With time the picture had faded and frayed around the edges, but was always displayed proudly in her tiny flat.

She often reflected on her life and would dwell on milestones that signaled failure to her. The anti-depressants provided by the local clinic didn't seem to help much. The only thing that kept her going was the occasional communication with her daughter, who had moved to Johannesburg. Grace was always hoping that her daughter would have the life that she had aspired for – a lovely house, a good husband, two cars and a few laughing, playing children. She was puzzled and grieved by the fact that her daughter never spoke much about her private life. Grace didn't know any of her friends or how she was doing at her job. Having sacrificed so much for her daughter, it was disconcerting not knowing whether it was justified.

Oh, Lord, I am weak, confused, and uncertain, but
I am hanging on to You, expecting relief.

The sad news reached her on a crisp and perfect day in Cape Town. The sunny sky and gentle breeze might have been heavenly, but the news was hell. She remembered the priests used to say that hell and paradise were brutally close together, but she had never understood it until that day. Her daughter had been kidnapped and her tortured, lifeless body was discovered after five days.

Grace spent the next day in church, which was the closest thing she knew to the Swedish school that she grew up in. She was inconsolable, trying to figure out why God had no mercy, and why her life meant nothing in the end. After several hours of desperation and nowhere to turn to, someone saw her and gave her a punnet of take-away food. She was not hungry and did not know what to do with it. She went into a corner of the church and wept. After a while she became aware of cats meowing next to her, a mother and her three kittens. Soon they were devouring the food. Grace fed bits and pieces to the cats and their delight at the unexpected feast made her forget, if only for a few moments, the dreadful tragedy.

Once again she lifted her hands to the cross and asked, why do I suffer so much? Once again there was no answer. Her attention went back to the kittens; making sure they ate what was left. She remained disillusioned about God not answering her prayer.

That night she slept deeply, exhausted by the shocking news. The Virgin Mary came to her in a dream. Grace had always loved the Mother of Jesus and felt that they shared a maternal instinct. Mother Mary said to Grace, "God's mercy, love and generosity are not based on what we want. And it is an illusion of yours that your suffering with drugs had been due to your lack of education and that that was what drove you to give your daughter an education. Sometimes what we think is the path of love and happiness, can be the very source of our misery."

In the morning she thought she needed a period of repentance to be fully available for God. She remembered the cats in the church and felt that it was a sign from God that she should start showing her compassion, love and light. She believed that it would be the only way to the contentment she was so deeply missing in her life.

She started working at the church and enjoyed the pleasant environment that it provided. One day she had an epiphany – she realized that anything worldly could be suspicious, but that God's light and endless generosity were always there, despite what we might think or experience. The smartly dressed businessman appears so rational and considerate, yet a deceitful wolf may very well hide inside him.

Grace became a respected and loved presence at the church. She was content with her destiny in life and joyfully lived her faith despite all the tragedies and uncertainties around her. She also reveled in her ever-growing circle of friends, and cats.

> *"Whenever I remember my troubles are over, I am content, and I have discovered all the wealth and treasures in that remembrance and my prayers to You."*

46
Uniformed Brutality

Looking through some old photo albums of our time in America, my son Hassan had pointed to a photo in which he recognized himself, and asked who else was with him in the picture. We were enjoying some family time before Hassan would leave the next day to begin his journey as an adult.

Hassan was about one and a half years old when the photo was taken and with him was Giorgio. They were both sitting on a red tractor, Hassan snug in front of Giorgio, smiling from ear to ear.

"Oh, that is Giorgio," I told Hassan. "He used to be a soldier who came to live with us for a while after he fought in the Vietnam War."

And suddenly the song 'Universal Soldier' by Donovan popped into my head as I drifted into old memories.

He's a Catholic, a Hindu, an atheist, a Jain,
A Buddhist and a Baptist and a Jew...

I could see Giorgio clearly in my mind's eye, such a pleasant young man with his burly Italian looks. Yet such a broken man. When we met him, sadness hung like a cloak over his shoulders.

As was the case with so many soldiers, he had returned from war deeply depressed and plagued by several ailments. During the war he was part of an elite strategic targeting team that used lethal high-tech systems and equipment which obliterated dozens of villages and killed thousands of people. At the time, he, like so many other young soldiers, believed that he was on a patriotic mission that was essential for world peace and prosperity. The depersonalisation of war made possible by the technology only enabled the war to escalate and for atrocities to be committed without ever seeing "the enemy" face to face.

... And he knows he shouldn't kill
and he knows he always will,
Kill you for me, my friend, and me for you...

A year after returning from Vietnam, Giorgio, who had been in his early twenties then, began to have doubts about the war and this manifested as bouts of fits that became ever more severe. He had been diagnosed with numerous disorders and received special medical treatments for veterans.

Some of the disillusioned soldiers converted to Islam in their quest for answers or some meaning of what happened to them and why they were made to do what they did. Two of these victims of a senseless war ended up on our farm and I grew very fond of them. They both shared an immense shock because they saw first-hand what humanity was capable of. They ended up staying with us for three years.

Giorgio was convinced that the chemical warfare had rendered him infertile. He desperately wanted to have a family one day, but thought that this part of the American dream would never come true for him. At the time our baby boy had just started walking and Gorgio attached himself to the little boy with fervour. They became inseparable and even started imitating each other's mannerisms. Giorgio was our driver and also supervised the construction on the farm, with his little companion always by his side. It was therefore no surprise when Hassan's first word was 'digger'.

Giorgio did marry eventually and even had children. A few years later he visited us and talked about the insights he had gained about humans and their propensity for war. He said that it was the formality of behaviour that was the curse of humankind. The moment you put on a uniform your attitude changes to adapt to the outer appearance. Whether you are soldier, a corporate person or an airline official, all these roles reduce your humaneness, and mask it to enable you to act in a manner that another human will consider unethical. In the name of some authority, you can perform brutalities that you could never have done if it was only you without the illusions of formality. It is this organised brutality in us that will probably bring about the end of the current life stream on earth.

When you have several people following a certain direction it attains an additional communal reality which nobody questions anymore. Despite this artificial feeling of being part of something great, everyone is actually only concerned about themselves and the age-old questions we all ponder. Who am I? Why am I here?

What am I looking for? What happens after death? But they are easily superseded by warped political ideals.

And he's fighting for democracy
He's fighting for the Reds
He says it's for the peace of all
He's the one who must decide
Who's to live and who's to die
And he never sees the writing on the wall …

47
The Empty Cradle

Latifa lived in the sprawling city of Karachi. She was a dedicated teacher and had a loving husband, yet, there was something missing. She yearned for a child.

She was thirty four and found herself starting to despair. The ticking clock of her fertility had cast a shadow over her otherwise peaceful life. Moreover the whispers of societal expectations were always around her. And the subtle fear that her husband might abandon her if the cradle remained empty for much longer took root in her heart.

Even though Latifa found solace in her faith, the worries wouldn't subside. She decided to do something about it and planned a pilgrimage to the shrine of Shabaz Qalandar, a Sufi saint buried in the desert of Sindh. She had heard that barren women would go there to pray for a child.

The Empty Cradle

The journey from Karachi to the shrine felt long and she wondered if she had made the right decision. The heat of the desert embraced her as she disembarked. She made her way to the shrine and felt a sense of awe as she entered the sacred space; a realm where time seemed to dissolve into the mystic atmosphere of devotion.

At the entrance of the shrine she found the shops that she had been told about so many times. They sold and rented tiny cradles crafted from local wood – symbols of hope and miracles. She rented one and as the sun dipped below the horizon she entered the shrine, looking for a place to sit down. The corridor was lined with rows of women with shared dreams and silent pleas. Surrounded with hopeful souls such as herself, she found a spot where she could spend the night. At first it felt somewhat awkward rocking the cradle and praying, but soon she got lost in the chanting around her and she yielded to her supplications.

Soon the full moon rose above the desert and in the stillness of the night, her heart opened to the boundlessness, seeking divine grace that would fill her empty arms with the joy of motherhood.

Latifa returned to Karachi and months passed, but still her cradle remained empty. The weight of unfulfilled desires lingered, yet the experience of her pilgrimage endured in her heart.

One day the doorbell rang, but when she opened the door, there was nobody. Then she heard a faint cry and looked down. At the doorstep was a box with a tiny baby in it. Shocked, she picked up the little bundle. A piece of paper fell from the blankets. It was a note addressed to her, imploring her to care for the baby girl as if she were her own.

In the face of this unexpected blessing, Latifa's heart swelled with a mix of emotions – joy, gratitude, and a profound understanding that the divine plan unfolded in mysterious ways. The child, a living embodiment of answered prayers, was proof of that.

As she embraced the little one, Latifa realized that the journey to the shrine had not merely been a quest for a biological child, but a spiritual pilgrimage. The cradle she rocked in the sacred corridor might not have held her biological child, but it held the miracle of motherhood in an unexpected form.

She named her Hiba, meaning God answered. In the quiet moments of nurturing the child, Latifa contemplated how love transcended the boundaries of biology. She became a mother not through blood but through the divine threads that connected their hearts. For the first time she understood that a prayer unanswered is not necessarily a prayer denied.

48
The Oldest Bridge in Baghdad

Whatever appears on earth, will also disappear.
Whatever is born, will also die.

Adil waits patiently for the group of tourists to disembark the bus. He is a very knowledgeable guide in the city of Baghdad, which, only a few decades ago, had been one of the most beautiful capitals in the East. Until the mid-thirteenth century it was also one of the greatest cities in the world.

Being built on the banks of the river Tigris, the city has no less than fifty five bridges and the group is on their way to a certain bridge, one of the oldest in the city. Adil tells them that this bridge is still an inspiration for many writers because of all the events that had taken place on it. They stop near the bridge at a spot with several benches and palm trees where people will often sit down reflecting on its rich, albeit tumultuous, history. Nowadays lavish weddings are held on or near the bridge, but its past is anything but festive.

The lively group gathers around Adil as he starts sharing a legendary story about the bridge.

"Very long ago, not too far from this spot, a young man had stood for hours, holding a large leather pouch of gold coins. He was waiting for the new ruler to pass by with all the usual pomp and ceremony. The deposed ruler, chained to his favourite horse, was being dragged across the bridge. His legs were tied to stones, and he was eventually pushed into the water. The new ruler and his entourage joyfully laughed and shouted, moving on until they reached the young man with the bag of gold. At great risk to himself, the young man stepped right in front of the ruler's horse and told him that the bag of gold was for him, as had been stipulated in his father's will. The new ruler was perplexed and asked who the young man's father was. 'You do not know my father,' the young man replied. 'He died a few years ago, leaving the bag of gold behind with the condition that the gold be given to the most foolish person on earth, because he would certainly need it. Today, Sir, you see your own destiny ahead of you, just like the previous ruler knew he would inevitably be deposed and killed, and yet you rejoice. Surely, you deserve this gold!' The young man handed the gold over and retreated as quickly as he could."

The tourists are enchanted by Adil's storytelling skills and encourage him to tell more.

"There are numerous anecdotes about how the river was used as a dumping ground for people whom the authorities wanted to be rid of. Like the Turkish ruler who sent chained prisoners with weights tied to their feet to be thrown off the bridge at night. Another story tells the sad tale of a beautiful princess who asked her two servant ladies to push her into the river to avoid her arranged marriage to a drug addicted prince. And then there is the story of Genghis Khan's grandson, Hulagu, who, when he conquered Baghdad, ordered tons of books to be thrown into the river so that horsemen could almost cross on a bridge of books. Legend has it that for months the river downstream ran murky black, stained by the ink."

As usually happens after these stories, the mood among the tourists have turned more sombre. Adil takes this opportunity to make his point that we are a people who don't have enough respect for the relics of the past. He emphasises the many beautiful archaeological items from the ancient past that had been deliberately destroyed or obliterated, partly due to superstitions or the illusion that they were part of idol worship. He talks about the ancient schools of learning and seminaries that had mostly vanished and how, after five centuries of Ottoman misrule, numerous barbaric and despotic autocrats completed the remaining destruction, bringing about untold misery on people and buildings. Out of millions of books and manuscripts, only a fraction survived the numerous sweeping armies, whose horses trampled over public and private libraries, most of which were set on fire.

As the tour group assembles on the bridge, Adil asks them to look down and imagine the river running black with the ink of thousands of books, making such a thick pile that it almost formed a new crossing.

"In time the books and ink were cleared away by the river itself and life was peaceful once more. Until it was time for another uprising, which led to the destruction of this bridge. The next regime rebuilt the bridge and today you are standing on the oldest bridge in Baghdad that is still in use, yet this bridge is only a few decades old…"

The life of an individual human being is not that different from a new city that is born, thrives, reaches maturity, then begins to decay and constantly needs repairs and improvements. Within us there are also bridges: physical, material, and emotional connections. We try to remember events that have caused us injuries, as well as those that brought us delight. Each one of us could be thought of as a new city that had died out, but its spirit carries on to inhabit a new one.

49
Doors, not Window

Susan sighed a big sigh of relief when the airplane touched down after the long flight home. She couldn't wait to see her family again after working in Australia for the past year. She was especially eager to see her younger brother again and looking forward to the two of them sharing their stories about their different explorations. Andrew had taken a gap year after finishing high school and went to work on a kibbutz.

Andrew, with his bright eyes and sharp, inquisitive mind; a golden boy, born to shine on life's fleeting stage.

But the moment she saw him, she knew something was very wrong. He had lost quite a bit of weight and was anxious and fidgety. He assured her that she was just imagining things and that he had never been better.

It was only after a few days that she managed to find some time alone with Andrew, who was behaving very differently from the day at the airport. He was extremely relaxed and spoke with an unfamiliar drawl. They were both sitting on her bed and she showed him the jewellery she had bought on her travels; an amethyst ring, a coral necklace, and her favourite, an opal stone with its multi-coloured hues. He looked at her condescendingly and said, "You don't know how much more beautiful they would look if you saw them while under the influence of drugs."

Susan caught her breath and then started questioning him relentlessly. What was he taking, wasn't he afraid of its long-term effects, and what about the distress his drug-use would cause their parents. But none of her entreaties touched his youthful arrogance. He laughed at her question about their parents, "They haven't got a clue," he sniggered. Andrew was clearly high. The drugs transported him effortlessly into a realm of heightened awareness where everything was possible. How could the pedestrian challenges of everyday life compete with this world with its infinite openings?

Of course the question 'why' also came up. "Because it feels good and it pays well," came Andrew's blasé answer. At that moment Susan realized that the problem was much bigger than she thought. Her brother wasn't just going through an experimental phase, he was actually involved in trafficking drugs as well. He even tried to persuade her to take LSD. "It will shift your perspective of the world and you will be much less critical and judgmental of others. It is like a heightened pure awareness," he said.

Susan decided to find out what this attraction to drugs was all about. She questioned all her friends. Some of them were just like her, they regarded them with deep apprehension and feared the unpredictability of its effects. Others were more laid-back and admitted to using some drugs occasionally. They did not think that a joint on the weekend was more harmful than a glass of wine with dinner. But there was one friend, Linda, who had always been wiser than the rest, who asked deeper questions and made Susan realize that Andrew might be looking for meaning in his life. Linda knew a holy man from Somalia who was known as a healer of hearts and bodies. Perhaps, this master could bring about a cure.

Surprisingly, it didn't take much to persuade Andrew to agree to see the healer. Susan suspected that he agreed just to get her off his back.

Andrew expected lectures, strict rules and constant supervision, but instead the healer was gentle and humble. He just talked to him and tried to explain to him why he got addicted to drugs in the first place. "There are two sides of every human being," he said. "One is the biological human in its earthly habitat, enshrouded with all its hopes and dreams. The human side is usually taken care of quite well. We feed and clothe ourselves and go to the doctor when we are sick. We shelter ourselves in houses and work hard every day to sustain ourselves. We also take care of our family and friends. This human, biological side of us is bound to space and time. It cannot function beyond it.

"But the other side, which I will call your spirit or soul, is the mysterious eternal power that gives us life. And this side of ourselves we neglect. This part is not confined to space and time and sometimes we get glimpses into the other zones of consciousness that this part of us is capable of entering. When we dream or when we hallucinate due to some medication, we realize that our consciousness can shift. And then we want more of that and so the intrinsic battle between the part of you that is eternally alive and cannot be contained, and the human part which is bound to physical life, starts. How can these two parts accept each other? The answer lies in the physical human part accepting that it was born to die, and with that knowledge the human mind starts asking questions about what happens when the body dies. That is one of the reasons why people will start using drugs; they want to find an answer to the question, what type of consciousness will we have when we die? We want a little peek into what comes next. Taking any mind-altering drug makes people feel as if they are touching those other zones of consciousness. But that is not necessary. It is like entering a house through a window instead of the door. Entering through a window is dangerous and it comes with the risk of injury."

"So, if the drugs are windows, then what is the door?" Andrew asked.

"That is very simple, my boy. The door is to enter just as you are. Just practice stopping any movement and thought and let your soul lead you to the timeless and boundless part of yourself. Then you are at the door of eternity. You don't need any drugs to experience that. It is the ultimate bliss, that emptiness, that silence."

"Is that all?" Andrew asked in disbelief. "I must just learn to sit still and be still?"

"Indeed, that is all," the healer said, smiling, "but it takes much more practice than you think. In the meantime I want you to stay for a while. There are certain things that can be taken in and comprehended through your ears, but true understanding comes by doing things, by sincere companionship, by seeing others' suffering and helping them. It would seal your healing if you follow me and help me with my work in the community. This will also give you time to face this addiction of yours head-on and change direction. If a car is going backwards, it cannot simply go forward again. You have to change the gear first. Stay here until you find the forward gear again."

To Susan's delight, Andrew returned some months later sober, and with the brand new addiction of making time each day to plug into the infinite.

50
Sakina House

For centuries Sri-Lanka accommodated different ethnic groups who lived side by side in small tribes. Although the groups lived separately there was no animosity, because they were very poor and at the time there was no central government. Hindus, Buddhists, Sinhalese, Arabs, Muslims and Christians existed peacefully side by side. Some groups were larger, like the Tamils, who were also Hindus. The Muslim population had grown considerably due to a few accidents. One such accident involved a Moroccan trading ship on its way to China that had been shipwrecked at the southernmost tip of SriLanka. A few hundred 'Moors,' as the North African Muslims were called, had been saved and the local ruler encouraged them to stay until their boat was mended. This happened a few more times and so, within a hundred years, a strong Moorish community had been established. By 1900 the Moors constituted about ten percent of the SriLankan population. When the civil wars started, the Moors were one contingency of the dispersed factions. In the past, they had been held together by basic survival, but once money, politics and influence from India entered the scene, their peaceful existence was ruined.

After the government troops attacked a small village in Sri Lanka, food, water and shelter were hard to come by. The army arrived before dawn looking for dissidents. Upon finding none, they vented their anger on women, the elderly and the young. Within an hour the army had looted whatever was usable and torched whatever was combustible. Edible domestic animals even disappeared.

A young mother and her two little daughters, barefoot in tattered clothes, were looking for anything salvable in the ruins of their house. The smell of burnt wood from the beams of the house mingled with the smoke from burning trees nearby. Stench and doom engulfed everything. The youngest girl began to sob loudly. Sitting on the charred earth, her mother hugged her, comforting her with a gentle swing of her knees. With a shaky voice she whispered to the girls, "Thank God, we were not raped or injured."

The father, Saheed, a hardworking Moor, like most men in the village, left a few months before in fear of raids and reprisals from the two ruthless factions, as well as numerous splinter groups and criminal gangs. He sent several messages to his family to reassure them that he was well. He had even sent the girls a few gold bangles, which were promptly sold and the money used for food and water.

Before the war he was known in the village as a person who served others. He had a strong connection with the unseen that he never talked about. There was a constant line of connection between his soul and his spiritual teacher, Zahida, who was recognized as an enlightened person by the Moors. Every night before he went to bed Saheed would pray and visualize his teacher with him. He would then ask her any questions he had for the next day. Each morning when he left the house, he would perform at least three acts of charity dedicated to her.

The war eventually came to an end, as all wars do, but not before much more violence and killing of innocent people.

Saheed was among the first to return. He had done surprisingly well by working on ships and came home with his savings. The disturbing state of his birthplace and the suffering of his people stirred something in him and after discussions with some elders, he declared that what he really wanted to do was to make a difference to people's lives. His idea to undertake a project that would bring out the best in people and give honour and dignity to the weak and the meek was greeted with enthusiasm by all present. He was adamant that it would not be based on any specific religion, as he believed that religion in the modern age could be divisive and bring discord to humanity.

A meeting with a few Buddhists and Muslims and a family of Christians was held. They all encouraged Saheed to embark on whatever was going to help rebuild the town and especially to assist the young people to carve out a better future.

A derelict house was restored to become a small factory for straw mat weaving. It was called Sakina House, after the Arabic word meaning 'peace'. Saheed's energy was focused on finding buyers in advance so that the mats could be designed to their specifications. Within a year or so, the village emerged from the ashes of warfare and was considered as an example of tolerance, cooperation and hope in the area.

As an unexpected bonus, something that caused the village much annoyance in the past – the deafening croaking of huge bullfrogs at night – became a very profitable business. A market for giant frog legs sprung up in France, where it was known by the bizarre term "Nymphs' thighs". Soon this unlikely delicacy became a good source of income for the villagers and peasants. It even started competing with the price of abalone and rare fish. So it happened that the frog leg craze hoisted Saheed to celebrity status in different parts of Asia.

When you exercise mercy and compassion upon earthly creation, the heavens showers greater gifts on you. When you allow goodness to flow through you, divine grace follows.

51
Sai Baba

The desire to believe in the eternal and boundless is a natural drive in human beings as it connects normal intelligence with the highest lights of intelligence.

During my wanderings in India there were a few beings whom I wanted to visit in the hope of understanding their awakened states.

Sai Baba of Shirdi, a nineteenth century Indian spiritual master honoured by Hindu, Muslim and other devotees, had been one of them. He had renounced everything that most people strive for, and he hardly ever spoke. I have tried to visit his grave a few times, unsuccessfully. But one day a friend made arrangements for me to go by car and meet a knowledgeable person in these matters at the graveyard. Unfortunately the trip did not take place because I had injured my back and traveling in a car was out of the question.

Many decades after Sai Baba of Shirdi passed away, another young man, also called Sai Baba, emerged. He became a very famous Indian guru with a considerable global following. He had an enormous afro hairstyle from which his face peered out very dramatically. I had the opportunity to visit his center near Bangalore twice.

His reputation of performing miracles included dematerializing and rematerializing objects. His signature miracle was producing ashes from his hands, which his followers would collect for meditation and healing purposes.

During my first visit I was especially intrigued by certain Indian sweets that Sai Baba would produce by just waving his hand. I also received a piece once and just before finishing the sweet, it occurred to me to take the last morsel to a forensic lab. While waiting for the results, I visited several sweet shops in Bangalore and ended up at one where I was informed confidentially that these sweets would just disappear from the shelves, but at month end someone sent by Sai Baba would come to pay for the missing sweets. The lab results showed nothing unusual about the ingredients of the sweets.

My second stay there was quite eventful. Several celebrities were visiting Sai Baba, including a famous musician called Ravi Shankar, who had been one of his followers. A week before Ravi Shankar was on a world tour and lost the golden locket that Sai Baba had given him on a previous visit. He was very distressed and as soon as he could, he made his way to Sai Baba to ask for a replacement. Early one morning he was taken to Sai Baba's cottage. Astonishingly, Sai Baba was holding the lost locket and chain in his hand for everybody to see. After this the atmosphere in the compound was highly charged and it confirmed to me that most human beings look for miracles and unusual events as a possible gateway to the unknown and to increase their faith and trust in the unseen.

When Sai Baba emerged from his cottage there were a few thousand people lined up in the compound, stretching for approximately two kilometres. The visitors had made a walkway so that Sai Baba could walk in the middle to greet them. I thought he would certainly give me a special welcome when he reached me, but this didn't happen. The voice of my ego said, 'he does not know, ignore it.' As Sai Baba walked, he stretched out his arm and from his cupped hand ash was pouring. People were dashing to catch some of it.

I had met several of Sai Baba's devotees before. They claimed that their prayer niches contained his picture and little shells containing this ash and that these shells would miraculously never go empty. I was truly amazed by the considerable amount of ash that poured out of his hand and onto the ground everywhere he walked.

My natural curiosity connected me to numerous stories and investigators who tried to disprove the miracle. When Sai Baba died, many articles and books appeared, mostly to denounce these miracles, but the majority of his followers remained staunch and convinced that he was an avatar – God's incarnation on earth.

52
The Prisoner

Rashad had served a two year sentence for some banking irregularities and was waiting to be released from prison. His family was already waiting eagerly outside. The friendly warden he had befriended saw him off him saying, "You are leaving this prison for a more depressing one. Every conscious being is in God's web and unless you know the magnificent governor of your new prison, you will remain discontent."

During Rashad's incarceration he had studied world religions and discovered the universal truths they shared. His conclusion was that you could never fully understand the real meanings of religions unless you were stripped from your own culture and judgments. Jesus alluded to life's sacredness, to respect everything that is alive. The Hindus also believe that everything that exists has a level of sacredness. From the Sufis he learnt that the microcosm resonates and reflects the macrocosm. From Vedism he understood that human beings are bound by fire, water, earth and air. Without fire there was no life and without air no growth. Real connectedness was due to water and earth. Earth was the cosmic dust and every human being carried within them all the elements that constitute matter. Having been born a Muslim, he also understood how profound the Qur'an was, but unless it was lived fully, no transformation could occur and religion would just became ritualistic.

> ***Every human being is composed of matter and energy, limited personal consciousness and supreme light.***

Four months before his release he gave a talk on the nature of existence and human duty. He emphasized that most religious paths try to describe the tangible, which was just the outer shell of an immeasurable cosmic reality not subject to space and time. He explained that it was necessary to transcend earthly limitations in order to catch a glimpse of this limitless Reality.

On a few occasions Rashad had experienced the light of God descending upon him with such force that tears just poured out. This led to the insight that tears are the soul's blood.

He emerged from prison accepting his individual identity, as well as the oneness of communities and societies that bonded through language, religion and kinship. He was filled with expectations and dreams of everything he would accomplish in his new life.

The day after his release a party was held in a luxurious house. The atmosphere was cheerful and most of his wealthy relatives and friends were there. But he was very solemn. He realized that he had also once been part of the frivolous life he now witnessed around him. Just as he had gathered the courage to talk to a partygoer about the spiritual nature of man, the host introduced a stand-up comedian to fill in time with jokes.

Rashad had often wondered how he could share his precious knowledge of the divine with others. He longed to show everyone that we are prisoners of our own illusions and fears and that the only way out was through the door of truth, which only opened inwards. He wanted to explain how superficial our lives were and that short-lived earthly contentment was the veil hiding the truth of the eternal and boundless light of life.

He missed the friends he had made in prison. Yusuf was a Jamaican drug merchant who, after four years in prison, seemed to have been reformed and was able to touch a higher zone of consciousness. The second friend was a politician from Nigeria incarcerated for numerous embezzlement charges. He had lived in London before his enemies managed to pin him down. The third friend was a young man named Yakoob, a Kurd from Iran who was recruited by a Western government's secret agency to spy on the government of Iran. In a strange twist the same agency denounced him as a spy. Yakoob had a pure heart and was very wise for his age.

A year went by and during the month of Ramadan Rashad prayed repeatedly for a new direction that would enable him to fully engage with life. No answer came. When the time of fasting ended, he received several invitations to Eid celebrations, but decided to go to the poorest mosque in Brixton instead. Most of his family and friends avoided the area, because the mosques were under constant surveillance for potential terrorists.

Rashad was ecstatic to find himself praying next to the recently released Yakoob and invited him for coffee at a nearby café. He asked Yakoob what he should do with his life and the answer was prompt and clear. "My grandmother used to say that whatever the problem is, near it lies the solution. You should be involved with people who have been incarcerated, like you and I. Men who have emerged with their inner light switched on. I will tell you where to find these men. Imagine a hundred people like us emerge from these prisons illumined to the vast truth that stretches beyond human limitations: that would be real human emancipation."

> *Life on earth is a beautiful journey for those who are awakened; and a depressing prison for those living as ego-selves.*

53
Warren Shaw

On a stormy summer's night in the Highveld two strong Afrikaner men were forcing their way through a rushing river, wading through mud and puddles, while carrying a midwife to the Shaw's farmhouse. Everyone remembered that storm, because the rain did not abate for a whole week and caused flooding in the whole area. It was also the night that Warren would be born.

His mother was a devout Christian and had the habit of interpreting various events as either signs of trouble, or gifts from the Creator. After Warren's birth she began to identify many signs about her son's future. She was certain that he would live a remarkable life.

Young Warren loved his Bible lessons and enjoyed singing in the church choir. His school days had been quiet and trouble-free, and he was loved by the staff and the other students. After matriculating he studied medicine, but halfway through his first year, he received a call from his father asking him to come home urgently.

It was a cold winter's afternoon, after coffee and rusks had been served in the kitchen of the family farm, when Warren learnt that his father was suffering from a severe muscular degenerative disease. His father begged him to come back to run the farm. Warren had no choice but to oblige. He was barely twenty when his father passed away peacefully.

Warren had always been curious about different world religions and, being a fruit farmer, this led him to explore what the scriptures had to say about fruit and herbs. He believed that fruits mentioned in scriptures would have special nourishing properties that others won't. He was particularly interested in figs and mulberries and found it fascinating that figs hide their seeds whereas mulberries expose them on the outside. He planted several varieties of each. Several types of songbirds love these fruit and Warren welcomed them. Soon he began a modest but successful dried fruit business.

He was also very interested in honey and studied the medicinal properties of different types. He found that a little honey in warm water taken at night was a good tonic for sleeping well.

Warren became an ardent advocate of eating only what is in season and what is produced locally. He became the chairman of the organic food association and established a company to produce and market organic fertilizers.

On the surface he had accepted the fork in the road he was forced to take when his father fell ill. Somewhere in his twenties he got married, but only a few months after his wedding his mother was diagnosed with cancer and she died before the year was over. Warren continued farming, and welcomed two children into the world.

In his thirties Warren had decided to give up farming, bought a house on the outskirts of Pretoria and relocated his family. His wife had planted a tree so close to their house that its roots began to lift the foundation. A few years later it caused a crack a few inches wide, but no amount of explaining and arguing could convince her to cut the tree down. One day, during a violent summer storm, the roof of the kitchen collapsed and his wife's leg was injured so badly that it caused her excruciating pain for the rest of her life.

After this incident, Warren seemed to lose interest in life and started drinking heavily. Some people who knew him speculated that he was longing to exchange earthly life for the afterlife.

The soul is beyond space and time, whilst the self on earth is on a quest for the permanent.

Warren believed in the afterlife and had always been curious about what the religious scriptures of the world had to say about it. He studied, amongst others, the Bible, the Qur'an and the Bhagavad Gita in order to satisfy his quest for information about life after death. He concluded that the best way to prepare for the afterlife was to let go of the illusion of having an independent will of your own, but rather to align your will to the will of the Divine. He believed you just had to surrender yourself to the role that presented itself at the moment it presented itself: opening the door for someone, feeding someone, or rescuing an injured bird.

In the end, earthly life held no attraction for him anymore. He was lost in a self-induced oblivion, while awaiting the ultimate oblivion.

54
The Heirloom

The calendar on Mika's smartphone reminds her that it is time to air the tablecloth again. She can hardly believe it has already been three months.

She goes to the drawer where she keeps the old Japanese silk tablecloth that has been in her family for several generations. She takes it out carefully from the cotton pillowcase, letting the cool, smooth silk run through her hands. The unusually large tablecloth used to be white as snow, but it has yellowed somewhat over the years. Her fingers traces the ridges of the embroidery, which makes the tablecloth somewhat impractical. If you are not careful where you place the crockery, it will easily tumble.

When she moved to Canada she thought of leaving it behind, just imagining the precious silk sailing across the Pacific Ocean made her heart twist. But she couldn't leave it. It would be like leaving a piece of herself behind. For Mika the tablecloth is a comforting symbol of tradition, a connection that transcends time and a bridge between generations. It is more than just threads and silk. It's a souvenir of a time when life was simpler, when crafting something by hand meant pouring your soul into it. And now that connection transcends borders, building a bridge between cultures and at the same time reminding her where she comes from. It's like a silent teacher, passing on the wisdom of patience, tradition, and love.

Her ancestors were Shinto, for whom purity, harmony and respect for nature are the utmost goals. They had probably sourced the silk from silkworms, spun in into thread and then woven the cloth from which the tablecloth was made. Months and months of embroidery followed, each stitch done with care and precision. She wonders how many people had a hand in creating it. A piece of her family's history is woven into the fabric, forever there.

Mika admires the craftsmanship of her ancestors, but she doesn't want to use the special tablecloth even though it is a utility item. Still it is a shame that such an exquisite item should be locked away in a drawer. It is as if the fabric whispers tales of ancient hands and dedication. She airs it out and lets it breathe a bit.

Suddenly a desire overcomes her to wrap herself in the tablecloth. She lies down on the carpet and carefully cocoons herself in it completely. The outside world left behind, she becomes aware of the intricate web of life that extends far beyond her own existence. It dawns on her that while her ancestors may have toiled to create this exquisite piece, they were also dependent on tiny creatures like silkworms for their livelihood. Humans and nature are so intricately interconnected and yet there is the notion in people's intellect of being independent, or self-reliant. It is such folly that we can be independent, no living entity can survive on its own. Just the other day she had read that the total biomass of insects on earth is seventy times more than the weight of all the people. Even the smallest creatures play a vital role in sustaining the delicate balance of ecosystems. Through the slits in her eyes she sees the dense network of threads in the fabric and her mind goes to spiders, the master weavers of the universe. She wonders how many people know that spider silk surpasses even steel in terms of tensile strength. It must have been from these seemingly insignificant creatures that humans have learnt how to spin wool, cotton and silk into fabrics that we use every single day. Blissfully Mika surrenders herself to the stories emanating of the tablecloth and gives thanks to nature for always sustaining her.

After a while she gets up, folds the tablecloth lovingly, slides it back into the pillowcase and returns it to the drawer. She replaces the lavender and rosemary to protect the tablecloth from pesky silverfish. With a fresh appreciation for her role as a steward of these interconnected threads of existence, Mika embraces her responsibility to cherish and safeguard the treasure for generations to come.

Mika's heirloom is a living legacy, a silent witness to the ebb and flow of time. And she is the custodian of its stories connecting the past with the future, carrying them across oceans and weaving them into the fabric of her own journey.

55

Barberton Gold

Gold is a physical entity, one of the hundred and eighteen known elements; and since its discovery thousands of years ago, it has been shrouded in myths and legends. It became incessantly sought-after by humans because they believed it will provide happiness and contentment.

Every child enjoys a treasure hunt. Every grownup hopes to find something precious. This hope of finding something rare and valuable is merely a reflection of the rarest of all treasures within every one of us – the human soul or spirit.

Decades ago local fortune seekers, as well as adventurers from abroad descended upon several locations in South Africa to prospect for gold and other precious stones. Many sites, including Pilgrim's

Rest and Barberton, still bear the earthly scars left behind by the relentless human quest for finding treasure.

One day a local friend took me to Pilgrim's Rest to show me the old cemetery where many gold-diggers, including his grandfather from Wales, had been buried. A few young prospectors had died from accidents, disease and fights. But what he was keen to show me were the graves of robbers and lawless miners whose headstones had been positioned in a different direction than the rest. In Barberton one can also witness this phenomenon.

More than a century ago Barberton became a destination for gold diggers. Alluvial gold had collected along the water channels over the millennia, leading to the earliest gold discovery in South Africa. It wasn't long before the mining activities in Barberton became an attraction, which necessitated a gold exchange office to be built. Naturally a residential club with a large bar followed soon after.

Some of the miners who struck it rich built English style homes, importing all the building material. One successful miner, whose house is now a museum, had even imported small portable coal irons so that the ladies' dress pleats would stay neatly in place while picnicking.

However, within a few decades most of the gold had been picked out and the small town returned back to its slow pace of farming and a few minor commercial and industrial developments.

At the end of the nineteenth century David Llewellyn from Cardiff in Wales was an active prospector in Pilgrims Rest. He had enjoyed relative success, enabling him to buy several other claims and employing a few workers. This triggered jealousy and unfounded accusations of dishonesty in his dealings. After a nasty fight at the door of the Royal Hotel, he died of knife wounds to his chest. He was buried in the local cemetery with his headstone positioned to indicate that he had been a robber.

A few decades later his great-nephew became a successful macadamia farmer and nut processor in Barberton. Sam Llewellyn was an influential member of the new generation of nut tree farmers, who relied on technology to combat bugs and other parasites. Sam had come to know that the headstone of his great-uncle's grave pointed in the same direction as those of known criminals. Sam decided to have the remains of his uncle exhumed and rebury him in Barberton with a new headstone. He also donated generously to the cemetery keepers and the relevant departments keeping records of deaths and burials. Sam was determined to leave a respectable name for the family, who now owned one of the largest macadamia operations in South Africa.

Many years later, destiny was to deal Sam a heavy blow. He, who had always worked hard to earn respect and build a good reputation, had to witness his much-loved only daughter, his pride and joy, fall in love and elope with an uneducated, unemployed refugee. This was hardly the son-in-law he had envisaged.

Sam had always considered himself a liberal Universalist, tolerant of all races and faiths, and was completely taken by surprise with the extent of his own prejudice and anger at his daughter's choice. He confided in a friend that this revelation, about how culture and upbringing can enmesh inescapable, deep-rooted human prejudices and judgments into our fibre, was worth more than all the gold in the world.

56
Awakened by Death

The sudden loss of Shahnaz's father in a tragic car accident left her world shattered. She had always thought the bond between them had been unbreakable, and now the void his absence created seemed insurmountable. Grief enveloped her, and with it came a flood of questions about life, death, and the mysteries beyond.

As a young girl, Shahnaz had been curious about death and often pondered over the afterlife, society's judgment on suicide, and the absence of euthanasia in religious laws. Dissatisfied with the stock answers she had received from those around her, she remained inquisitive, seeking to comprehend the unknown.

Her father's untimely departure intensified these questions. She couldn't accept that she would never see him again, and the yearning to communicate with him just one more time was an unquenchable thirst. A mourner at the funeral offered a glimmer of hope, suggesting that if she prayed sincerely enough, she might see her father in a dream and have an opportunity to ask him these pressing questions.

Months passed, but the dream she longed for remained elusive. Frustrated and desperate for answers, Shahnaz decided to visit an ashram where an Indian saint renowned for bridging the gap between the living and the dead resided. The saint told her that she should continue praying, but that she should be aware that she might not receive the dream she so longed for.

Staying at the ashram for a week, she immersed herself in prayers and contemplation. She finally had a dream, however it wasn't her father who appeared, but an uncle. He spoke of the interconnectedness of life and death, assuring her that the departed were not truly gone. He conveyed that life, sacred and everlasting, was a gift from the Ever-Living, and that death was a transition, not an end.

Still not satisfied, she approached the saint at the shrine, sharing her experiences and doubts. The saint, a wise and compassionate soul, acknowledged the limitations of the unseen and the inherent gaps in human understanding. He explained to her that the problem with much of the readings into the unseen was that they only contained a touch of reality. There were often gaps and those gaps rendered such readings unreliable.

The saint suggested exploring the teachings of Buddhism on death, emphasizing the importance of being prepared for the inevitable. Shahnaz, open to any avenue that might provide clarity, delved into Buddhist philosophy. The teachings, offering a perspective that transcended religious boundaries, resonated with her. Shahnaz learned that embracing the impermanence of earthly life allowed for a deeper appreciation of each moment and a more profound acceptance of the inevitable transition into the unknown. She came to understand that she didn't need to fear death, since it was simply a transition into a new zone of consciousness.

In time, Shahnaz discovered that, while the pain of her loss never truly vanished, it could coexist with a profound appreciation for the miracle of life. The ever-living essence, the sacred thread connecting past, present, and future, became a source of solace and a reminder that, in embracing the impermanence of life, one could find peace amidst the inevitable uncertainties.

57
Qalandari Baba

The universe is alive and responsive at multiple levels of energy.

A friend of mine from Islamabad phoned to say that something remarkable had happened whilst he was on a train in northern Pakistan. Somebody was sitting across from him reading a book, and on the back of the book was a photo of someone who had looked just like me. It was the biography of a wandering Sufi known as 'Qalandari Baba.'

A Qalandari is a wandering dervish, someone with no possessions, who never stays in one place for long and lives on trust.

Some people claimed that Qalandari Baba had been around for many decades, while others said that he first appeared a few hundred years ago. My friend was intrigued because he honestly thought the picture on the cover of the book was me. He thought I might have died and that somebody had written a book about me.

He told me that this Qalandari Baba had come to a suburb of Karachi where a small centre near a well was set up for him. He was known to do healing with water and many people would visit this well to fetch water and to receive healing from him. He was a very quiet man, always sitting in silence by the well. He had a companion who was always close by, looking after him.

I travelled to Karachi a few years after that, but by the time I arrived there, he had just passed away. I met his companion, who said that he was expecting me, even though he didn't know me. He wanted to tell me the story of how he had met Qalandari Baba. He told me that he was a successful building contractor when he first met him. He was fascinated by this quiet man, just sleeping anywhere, under a tree or behind a rock. He discovered that Qalandari Baba had another energy or power around him that was not normal, nor was it strange in any unworldly way, but inexplicable things would regularly happen wherever he was. I asked for an example.

What you desire, is already near you.

One day they had walked quite far and were getting very hungry and tired. They saw a few chickens scratching around small mud huts nearby. Qalandari Baba pointed to the chickens and said, "You would like to eat those chickens, isn't that true?" His companion agreed that a good lunch would indeed be very welcome. Qalandari Baba replied, "The chickens you want are not these ones you see, in fact, it is already being cooked for you. Just stay here and wait." Within half an hour two women came out with some trays, including one with two scrumptiously cooked chickens. They said that when they saw the two men arriving, they knew that they were Godsend and had to honour them as their guests.

The companion also told me that his life was turned upside down when he began to walk around with Qalandari Baba and started to take care of him. He completely lost interest in his work, his family, in everything, except in seeing how the seen and unseen connected in a seamless way. Not in a way that people might think or expect; it was different. It was another zone of consciousness, not the one we are used to, even though it was connected with the customary zone of consciousness. He said that if one could truly switch on to that other zone by switching off the customary zone, you could really live a life of miracles. Switch off your reason, your intellect, and your curiosity. Switch off humanity and divinity will take over. They are, after all, inseparable – humanity draws its energy from divinity. The companion told me that he had wanted to take care of Qalandari Baba's burial and expressed a wish to build a mosque in his honour.

Soon after Qalandari Baba's death, stories began to emerge about him, who he was and what miracles he performed. Within a few months considerable donations came in to build the mosque. A modern architect drew up the plans and it became a beautiful place for people to pray.

I went back to visit the mosque once it was completed. I wanted to pray there and had a deep desire to connect with Qalandari Baba's soul. I switched off and tried to induce some sort of exit from myself. I began to chant softly and when the energy of the trance took hold of me, I felt his presence. I didn't say anything, but he read my curiosity. I heard his voice asking me, "You are curious about my opinion on this building, not so? I never had any position. I would always just wander from one place to another. Only when I died and my body was gone, all this was built, people coming to honour me. Well, that is their mentality, they are people of matter and material and stone. That is what they know. And this is their zone of consciousness, and this might even lead them, slowly but surely, to another zone."

I also wondered whether Qalandari Baba was content about it all. It was such a magnificent place, modern and clean. His answer was, "It is not me, there is no me. It is the flow of intelligence, going back to its origin, to divine intelligence. I have no concern about the mosque and the visitors, it is not my business. When I was alive my business was to not fall into the illusion that I have an independent will and I followed that. Now I am there, where there is no independence, only interdependence."

58
Omar, the Silent

In a small Indian village nestled between the hills, a three-year-old boy named Omar had stopped talking. After much coaxing and even threatening, his family eventually sought the guidance of Shaykh Musa, a revered dervish known for his healing powers and insight.

When Shaykh Musa arrived at Omar's home the anxious family took turns recounting the story of how the once-vibrant child had suddenly stopped speaking after the untimely death of his mother. The grief-stricken family attributed his silence to the sinister influence of a djinn, believing it had taken possession of the young boy.

The Shaykh listened patiently for a while, but then silenced everybody and explained to all present that the cause of the boy's refusal to speak was clear: the shock of his mother's death had just been too much to bear and he felt overwhelmed with grief. The explanation left most of them relieved but others doubted his assessment. The Shaykh also understood that people in the rural villages would sooner blame something supernatural for their ailments than seeking a more rational answer.

In an effort to guide the family towards understanding, Shaykh Musa decided to address the broader issue of djinn. He gathered the villagers and began teaching them about the nature of consciousness and the pitfalls of our insatiable curiosity. "Human consciousness," he explained, "is but one of countless beams that radiates from life. If we accept our limitations, we will grasp the full story of existence, connections, relationships, beginnings, and ends within the relative limitations of our consciousness."

He spoke about the myriad realities existing beyond our comprehension. "There are many other realities and other types of consciousness, including the djinn. It is only courteous of us to contain our curiosity and refrain from interfering," Shaykh Musa emphasized. "We have not even sorted out the amazing state of our human conditioned consciousness, and yet, we are curious about djinn and angels."

Turning his attention back to Omar, Shaykh Musa urged everybody to shower the boy with love and to pray for him daily. He assured them that no exorcism was necessary, for his silence was a response to grief, not a malevolent spirit. He emphasized the importance of providing a caring environment that would allow healing in its own time.

The Shaykh decided to stay in the village for a while to assist the community on their path to spiritual awakening.

As days turned into weeks, Omar's family followed Shaykh Musa's guidance diligently. The boy was enveloped in love and slowly but surely, signs of improvement began to appear. Within a few months Omar started speaking again. It was a moment of profound joy, a testament to the healing power of love and compassion.

As Shaykh Musa bid farewell to the village, his memories of his own childhood flooded back. He recalled the pain of losing his own mother at a tender age and the silence that had gripped his soul for more than a year. Day to day life had been tedious and bleak. The connection between his own experience and Omar's struggle resonated deeply within him.

In that quiet moment of reflection, Shaykh Musa realized that sometimes the greatest exorcism is not the banishment of malevolent forces, but the unravelling of internal grief. In sharing his wisdom, he had not only helped to heal a young boy, but also guided an entire community towards a better understanding of the human state. He hoped that the shroud of fear that once enveloped the village would leave.

59

Murder at Bari Imam

Many years ago, Bari Imam had escaped the tyranny of a local Punjabi king and took refuge in a cave up the Margala hills, near present day Islamabad, now the capital of Pakistan. This was long before there were any villages or towns nearby. After his death, the shrine of Bari Imam became a destination for wandering dervishes and pious seekers of God, but also other ruffians and even prostitutes. This went on for centuries.

The shrine was on the old trade routes linked to the ever famous silk route. The area produced various fruits, and also opium. The spiritual carefree atmosphere of the location also attracted dangerous thugs. A local Sufi Shaykh, realizing that the shrine was being desecrated, asked one of his energetic devotees, Rajah Sahib, to take up residence next to the shrine and cleanse the place from any malevolent actions or people.

Rajah arrived with a few followers, armed with an absolute determination to please his Shaykh. A small hut with a reception room was built for him. This was soon followed by three guest rooms with en-suite bathrooms.

Within a few months some educated bureaucrats, army officers and government informers began to arrive to visit Rajah Sahib. His gentleness and hospitality had become known to all around. Within a few years the area around the shrine were cleaned up and the number of drug dealers and prostitutes were greatly reduced. Several government agencies began to assist and with their donations the project of shrine building in the area began to expand. An enormous tree shaded the shrine for as long as anybody could remember.

Unfortunately, as time went by, doubts, rumours and gossip also began to spread as to Rajah's real purpose. Some of his friends urged him to employ security guards, as people in such remote areas had been known to take the law into their own hands. He outright refused, saying, "We are from God and unto God we shall return."

Rajah Sahib's habit was to walk around the entire premises every morning, giving instructions to the dozen or so paid workers and other volunteers. One morning, as he stepped out of his cottage, three men approached him with greeting postures and then one of them opened fire. Seven bullets pierced Rajah's chest and skull. Within seconds he died on the dirt road in a warm pool of blood.

Just the day before Rajah had said to his friend, a university professor, that if he were to be assassinated, Allah's justice would take its course much more efficiently than the Pakistani courts.

Soon after Rajah's burial, the ambience of the shrine and the tree began to morph into a grand religious edifice. Within six months the long halls were filled with peasant families picnicking on the marble floors, feeding the numerous cats and kittens.

As for the murder case, a few dozen suspects were summoned in and out of the court with no indication as to when justice would be done. One morning a sweeper in the shrine dropped her broom and ran to the gate, screaming and howling for help. She had found a man's lifeless body floating in the fountain. He was identified as Mas'ud, one of several men receiving and managing donations for the shrine.

The next day Mas'ud's brother appeared at the university and handed a crumpled note to Rajah's friend, the Professor. It revealed that Mas'ud couldn't bear to live any longer after killing Rajah. He murdered him because he had been embezzling local donations to the shrine and was afraid of being discovered. But, ever since the murder, Rajah Sahib had appeared to him in vivid dreams every night and also haunted him during the day, asking him to show his empty hands and pockets. His life on earth had become such a misery that he could no longer take it. The note also explained how Mas'ud had avoided suspicion by bribing a court clerk to keep him out of the suspect pool. The clerk needed the money for a dowry that he had to pay urgently, because his bride-to-be had fallen pregnant.

The Professor eventually wrote a book containing Rajah Sahib's biography and the history of Bari Imam.

60
Indignant Indigenous

The graduate students at Boulder University in Colorado were hosting their Native American friend, Indignant Bull. He visits the college regularly, usually bringing a bag of trinkets, like small shaped and carved stones and crystals. He would lecture on the history and uses of these objects and also sell them to the students. His turquoise stones were particularly popular and pricey.

The city of Boulder is known for a few things. One of them is that the famous herbal tea company 'Celestial Seasonings' was founded there. They also boast some of the best kite shops in the world. Turquoise and other high-quality semi-precious stones and crystals can be found in nature there. Indignant Bull's uncle has a beautiful art emporium just outside the city, where you can find an array of stones and crystals, some in their natural form, some slightly modified or carved into a special shape. These stones are often used for healing. The shop is very successful, mostly because since the dawn of the New Age, it became very fashionable for educated, well-off people to buy and collect these stones and crystals.

Today Indignant Bull is being quizzed about nature and environmental degradation. An eager student asks, "Why are we so negligent, careless, and insensitive to Mother Earth?"

Bull does not answer immediately. Instead, he is quiet for at least a minute, then starts chanting to evoke the good spirits. His answer comes softly. "Are you sensitive to what your body tells you? Have you greeted your liver this morning? If you don't listen and respond to your own body, what chance is there that you are aware of what earth tells you?"

The hall falls quiet. After a while some of the students join Bull in chanting. Then someone else asks the next question, "How can we deal with the global ecological crisis?"

Bull speaks with immense deliberation, almost whispering. "Ecology needs to be treated as a spiritual reality, not simply as a natural event. We are guests on earth and until we honour our host, we shall remain confused, insecure and abusive towards nature. There is a huge lack of respect for life and biodiversity. Every living thing, big or small, deserves our respect. We can't go around destroying small living things, like insects, or even viruses. We need to have reverence for life as part of the overall mysterious miracle of the Big Bang and the emergence of life. It has taken the earth billions of years to become what it is now. But within a few thousand years we have made such an imprint that the consequences are irreversible. Therefore, everything we do from now on will bring about more complexities, more uncertainties and more fear. We have made our little earth a prison and the atmosphere is poisoned at every level.

We are looking for miracle cures all the time to prolong life, which also means prolonging human suffering.

"Life is the ultimate treasure, the gift from the unseen. Whatever is alive deserves to be respected to play its part in the overall orchestration of this tiny little earth of ours."

61
The Green Man

The book launch was a success. The author, famous for his charm as much as for his literary achievements, had kept the audience spellbound as he expounded on the many adventures he had had during a lifetime of travelling the world seeking spiritual enlightenment. 'Beyond Space and Time' was tipped to be another bestseller. Ricardo was seated in the bay window of the Edinburgh book store, which also resembled an antique shop because of all the Middle Eastern art on display. A ceramic rendering of the Bektashi dervish's begging bowl decorated one of the walls and the floors were covered with Persian rugs and kilims. It was a fitting setting for a writer who was known for his esoteric works.

He was signing copies while engaging in conversation with the ebullient customers. A bespectacled young man, book in hand, looking quite serious, approached him hesitantly and asked, "Ricardo, can you tell me about the person who has made the most impact on your life?"

Ricardo looked up, ran his fingers through his thick white hair, smiled thoughtfully and answered, "Of course. Come, sit down and I will tell you.

"He was the most remarkable man I have ever met, but his appearance was so ordinary, his demeanour so quiet and reserved that you could be forgiven for passing him by without noticing him.

"When I was a young man working on my first book, I had rented a cottage in a picture postcard village next to the Tweed and used to spend my days, notebook in hand, sitting on the river bank waiting for inspiration. One afternoon there was an elderly man fishing on a rock nearby my favourite spot, but I did not talk to him for fear of breaking my creative momentum. But then a sudden gust of wind lifted my precious notebook with its months' of scribblings and carried it into the water. Without a thought for my personal safety, I plunged into the water, swimming towards the floating notebook. The water was icy and my legs began to cramp. The current was too fast and I began sinking rapidly. A watery grave seemed likely to cut short my budding literary career. Suddenly I felt strong arms around me, dragging me to safety. Within a few minutes I was lying on the shore, a cold, damp bundle, having the water pumped out of my lungs by my rescuer. When I came to I saw that he was none other than the elderly fisherman whom I had spotted earlier.

"He insisted on accompanying me to the cottage. As we walked, I lamented the loss of my precious notebook. He replied assertively, "You were stuck, going over the same ideas again and again. It was a wind from God that blew away your misconceptions and has left you free to write something more original and meaningful.

"My rescuer left me at the cottage door, declining my invitation to come in. I thanked him profusely and asked for his name. 'People usually call me Kay, John Kay,' he replied. When I expressed the wish to see him again, he said rather cryptically, 'Don't worry, our paths will cross again.' With that he ambled down the road, leaving me bemused by the afternoon's events. I took in his appearance to ensure I would recognize him again. He was clad in fishing gear, wearing an olive green anorak and Wellingtons. He was tall and thin with a neat grey beard, aquiline features and piercing brown eyes.

"The man was right. Within three years my first bestseller had been published. The brush with death that afternoon in the icy waters of the Tweed changed my whole trajectory. Instead of writing a novel to emulate my literary hero, Camus, I embarked on a journey to discover the meaning of life. It was a life of a spiritual tourist, meeting diverse masters from different spiritual paths. In Japan I sat at the feet of a Zen Master, in India I spent time with a Hindu Guru, and in Morocco, a Sufi Shaykh. Once I had discovered the similarities in the inner meaning of their teachings and that the outer differences merely reflected their various cultures, I was inspired to write 'Unity in Diversity'. As you know that book gave me my first break and enabled me to devote my time to writing and reflection.

"Five years later Mr. Kay reappeared in my life while I was vacationing in Mallorca. Sipping a cappuccino in a cafe at the marina in Palma, I suddenly heard a scuffle and saw two policemen dragging an old man into their vehicle. Imagine my surprise when I recognised the old man as Mr. Kay. I ran after the police car but was too late to stop them. I was convinced there had been a dreadful mistake. Whatever could this harmless elderly gentleman have done to merit such harsh treatment? I hopped into my car and followed them.

"They stopped at the main police station in Palma. From my car I saw them lead Mr. Kay into the station. By the time I had parked and followed them in, the policemen were in the process of booking their prisoner. Mr. Kay was not protesting his arrest and seemed quite calm. 'Officers,' I exclaimed indignantly, 'I know this man and can vouch for him. You must have made a mistake!' 'Oh, no Señor, no mistake,' one of them responded. 'This man was caught damaging our King's yacht. We had to take him into custody and find out whether he is involved in any terrorist activities or whether he is some crank acting alone.'

"Mr. Kay shook his head and looked at me in the manner of a schoolmaster accustomed to the limitations of his pupils. 'Ricardo, isn't it? I told you we would meet again. Congratulations on your book, a valuable contribution to seeing beyond the differences of religions and cultures. Much better than that pretentious novel you had set your heart on writing. You do not have to worry about me. I happen to know that some Basque terrorists have planted a bomb on the yacht and it would explode once it was out to sea. So I damaged the controls of the boat, allowing them time to find the bomb, thus preventing a far worse accident. They will find the device later today and I will be out of here by tomorrow. Mind you, nothing wrong with a spot of incarceration. It brings a breathing space from all the trivia of daily living and everything that distracts you from the real purpose of being. Solitude and confinement are what people fear most. Both states break the connectivity in their lives and the illusion of personal freedom.'

"Dumbfounded I left the eccentric Mr. Kay to his day in jail and hoped that he was right about how events would unfold. First thing the next morning I rushed to the police station to enquire after him. A baffled officer told me that Mr. Kay had been right about the bomb and that it had been safely removed. But when the officers went to question Mr. Kay about how he had known about the existence of the bomb, they found an empty cell, the door ajar. Their prisoner had vanished into thin air.

"Our third encounter was in Morocco. I was driving through the mountains of the Middle Atlas to find a community of Sufis where Shaykh Ali, a man of immense light, knowledge and spiritual power, resided. Across the horizon I saw a small hamlet and drove towards it. The local Berbers were unfriendly, suspicious of the foreigner arriving in their midst. I was looking for someone to point me in the direction of Shaykh Ali's Centre. An old man, dressed in a faded green djellaba, was filling a hole near the entrance of a house. It was Mr. Kay. 'It's you again!' I exclaimed. 'What are you doing in this godforsaken place amongst these uncouth characters? And why are you helping the locals with road maintenance? A more undeserving bunch could hardly be imagined!'

"Mr. Kay shook his head. 'Well,' he said 'I see you haven't learnt much since we last met. Had I not warned you about typical human judgements? There is a box of old gold coins buried under this ditch. If I don't fill it up, the orphans, whose inheritance it is, will lose the treasure to their greedy uncle. By filling the hole, I should protect the cache long enough for the children to grow up and find it for themselves. By the way, take a left turn when you leave the village, drive for ten minutes or so uphill and you will find the Sufi Centre.'

"I reached the Centre at sunset to a warm welcome from the Shaykh's followers. It was a relief after being confronted by the unfriendly villagers. I had come with an introduction from Hashem, one of Shaykh Ali's pupils residing in Fez, and they were expecting me. We feasted on lamb and couscous, followed by intoxicating chanting. Later in the evening Shaykh Ali joined us. He was a being of light and I vanished into the warmth of his embrace. That evening time stopped for me and all my preoccupations faded into naught. For the first time in my life I entered the eternal 'now'. Here was the bliss of the moment I had read about but never experienced.

"I explained to one of the students how I had been lost and how an old man, whom I had encountered several times previously, had suddenly appeared and directed me to the centre. On hearing this, the Shaykh nodded knowingly and said, 'Khidr.'

"But who or what was Khidr?"

"This puzzle remained with me until my return to London, when I received an unexpected parcel in the post. It was a letter from Hilary, an elderly lady, who owned an antique bookshop I often patronised. She said she could no longer carry on with the business and was clearing out old stock. She had come across a book she thought might be of interest to me and in gratitude for the custom I had given her over the years she was gifting it to me. The book came with the instruction that it should only be taken out of its wrapping when I needed an answer to a crucial spiritual question. I ripped the package open immediately. The book was entitled 'Khidr, the Eternal Guide.' You can imagine my astonishment. At last I would learn who Khidr was."

By now a large group was surrounding the author, listening attentively to his captivating story. "The book," Ricardo said, "explained how Khidr, often known as the Green Being, first appeared in the Epic of Gilgamesh. He is also associated with the Biblical Prophet Elijah. Later the Qur'an reveals his meeting with the Prophet Moses. Khidr is the keeper of the secrets of immortality and the hidden catalyst for the spiritual transformation of mankind. He is associated with renewal, fertility and the colour green. It is said that in particular he helps people in danger of drowning or those lost in the desert.

Many Sufi poets have written about him, including Rumi. They say that he lives where the two planes of existence meet – the space with boundaries and the boundless space, the time that ends and the timeless. For humans to transcend the material realm of space and time, they need the help of Khidr, who can appear in more than one place at a time and assume many disguises."

The young man who had sparked off this whole dialogue became very passionate on hearing the story of Khidr. "So it was Khidr who inspired your books! I just read 'Beyond Space and Time.' You write about the meeting between the Prophet Moses and Khidr and this made me realize that there is a greater knowledge beyond our concepts of good and bad, truth and justice. You quote the story from the Qur'an where Khidr warns Moses that he must not question his actions, but when Moses sees Khidr making a hole in a poor fisherman's boat, thereby killing a boy, and building a wall to conceal buried treasure, he cannot contain himself. Then Khidr explains to Moses how none of these events were what they seemed, and that his judgements sprouted from his limited awareness and earthly perspective."

"You are quite right," replied Ricardo. "It was Khidr who guided me in my writings and in my search for meaning. Sometimes I feel he is like a puppet master pulling the strings of my life. Moses was a prophet and an arbitrator of human justice, but he knew the limitations of his earthly existence and that Khidr had access to Divine Knowledges beyond normal comprehension. Khidr became his Master and only by submitting himself to his authority could Moses learn from him. But like all pupils he failed the initial tests.

"It was from Khidr I learnt that unless we transcend our mental limitations, our judgement will always be limited."

62
The Medical Rep

You need to be humbled by mistakes, so celebrate your errors.

Donning a crimson cape, Kamala stepped out of her expensive car, her elegant legs accentuated by eye-catching high heels. Her colleague followed her carrying three pizza boxes. They walked confidently into the doctor's surgery. With seductive charm, she presented the very latest products from a big drug company, backed by scientific data in glossy pamphlets. She claimed that these new medications could produce miraculous results. The mesmerized doctor couldn't resist giving in. He accepted the samples and promised that he would prescribe them. Kamala's beauty and sunny personality, the scrumptious pizza and the rather useless gift of a paperweight shaped like a hippopotamus overwhelmed him. He received visits from representatives of drug companies regularly, but there was something about her that made his defenses crumble.

The sales and marketing department of this company knew how to entrap and enchant. Daily reminders in her diary prompted Kamala to maintain contact with all her prospective clients. She knew intuitively how crucial it was to make the doctor believe in his own importance. She was very successful in her endeavors. The hapless doctors were under a spell and would try to convince their patients that they needed the drugs from the company Kamala represented.

In her late thirties she became the mistress of an older doctor. But within a few months he was sued for malpractice and suspended from practicing for a year. Much of his savings was lost to his wife and legal fees.

At that time Kamala also realized that her youth was fading, and she took a job with an Indian mining family. She ended up marrying one of the young men of the family. She took to Hindu life effortlessly; she loved the gold embroidered saris and enjoyed the Hindu chants. After ten years of an enchanted life and two children, she began to take a serious interest in the family's charity work. She concentrated on the charities involved with building clinics, schools, and frail-care facilities for the elderly.

In her mid-fifties she was approached by Janet, a Canadian author, who wanted to write her life story. Janet was interested in successful charities all over the globe, and also in Kamala's spiritual life and insights. Janet was enthralled to learn about Kamala's days as a rep, but as she started telling her story, Kamala suddenly felt very ashamed that as a young girl she had used her looks to further her career. It felt as if that girl was a total stranger whom she no longer recognized.

Janet consoled her by reminding her that all men were children at heart and susceptible to flattery and special attention. Women can be very efficient in exploiting that trait, but they can also be equally efficient at being dedicated to an ideal. Women will often look for a worthy cause to serve and make a difference in other people's lives. Both men and women want to be appreciated, respected and honored.

In truth
all choices and desires
end up as one choice
the best
the most appropriate
the perfect match
the right link
in the chain of time,
emanating from timelessness
and returning to the eternal.

63
Maha, the Bahá'i Iranian

On earth the human soul is challenged with dualities in preparation for the return to Unity.

Maha was born into a wealthy Bahá'i family living in an affluent district north of Tehran. With many relatives and friends and the education she had had at the American school, she looked at life with a cheerful disposition. She had many Muslim friends, but by the time she was seventeen years old, Manoucher was her favourite and she started to imagine a future for the two of them together. They were part of a circle of friends who felt secure about their future due to their skills and training, as well as their higher status in the community. They had a comfortable and easy life, and no one could have imagined that within a few months, they would end up as refugees or in jail.

When the Iranian Revolution started and the Shah left, the writing was on the wall. Life for many wealthy people was turned upside down. A thunderous knock on the door was followed by interrogation and arrests. Maha's relatives and friends tried to rescue what they could and ended up being scattered all over the globe. Maha managed to get onto a flight to London, as there were no visa requirements.

Her father stuffed her suitcase with two valuable Matisse paintings, which he had bought for a few million dollars a few years before. While unpacking her suitcase in London, Maha discovered that one of the paintings had been badly damaged by a broken bottle of hair tint formula. The next day she contacted an art dealer, who referred her to a restorer who could fix the painting before her father would learn about the disaster. To her horror, the price of restoration was way above her means.

A telephone call from her aunt shattered her fragile composure and any hopes to adjust to her new life. Her aunt told her that several of their close relatives were in jail and others were scrambling to get out of Iran. The news about Manoucher was also bleak. His father had been an assistant to Hoveyda, the toppled prime minister, who was also a Bahá'í. As the revolution got more out of hand, executions became a daily occurrence and Hoveyda did not escape it.

A few days later the news about Manoucher grew worse. He had disappeared and no one knew where he was. Maha was inconsolable and tried in every way she could to find reliable information.

Meanwhile, her family was trying to get her enrolled into a private college in London. Other relatives and friends who had also landed up in England were beginning to regain some confidence in life.

Maha's wealthy cousin had invited herself to stay for a few days while her apartment was being renovated. To Maha's shock, she discovered that the reason for her cousin's frequent sleepiness and incoherence had been an addiction to morphine.

Then, to her great relief and surprise, Manoucher telephoned from Karachi to say that he and a few friends had managed to get across the border to Pakistan, having bribed their way. However, they had no means of getting any further. During the next few weeks, Maha became very gloomy and depressed. The rainy, dismal weather increased her yearning for Iran's bright sun. She started thinking that she should try some of her cousin's morphine, but she didn't know how to administer the injection.

The next day she took a walk in the park nearby and felt almost faint with melancholy and confusion. The cold drizzle drove her back to the apartment, only for her to realize that in her state of mind, she hadn't taken the key with her. She knocked and shouted to her cousin to open the door, but there was no response. Frustrated, she decided to call the concierge who had a spare key. To her horror, they found her cousin dead on the floor.

At the funeral the next day Maha met Parivash, a middle-aged lady who just came back from her annual pilgrimage to Israel where she had visited the shrine of the revered Bahá'i prophet, Baha'ullah. Maha felt that Parivash was sent by the heavens to give her hope and comfort. She told wonderful stories about the international Bahá'i communities and their support for one another. Millions of dollars were made available to assist their displaced followers all over the world.

In the days that followed Maha made up her mind to forget her past and to become a volunteer to serve the Bahá'i people. She was looking forward to be a citizen of the world, rather than a Bahá'í exile from Iran.

A year later she was enrolled in the University of Bristol, studying History. The news from Manoucher remained bleak and intermittent. He was idling his days in Karachi with no hope for the future. Maha took the courage to ask him if he was willing to convert to the Bahá'í faith, for if he did, she knew of funds for political exiles. Quite astonishingly, Manoucher told her that he would convert to anything just to get out of Pakistan.

With considerable help, patience and manipulation of facts and events, Manoucher eventually made it to England. To their surprise their previous interest in each other had waned. What they now had in common was helping relatives and friends who were still in hostile countries. Within a few years of lacklustre life in England their relationship had become a thing of the past.

A decade or two later, they had lost touch completely. They sometimes met at Bahá'í functions or family events. Manoucher had put on a lot of weight and was obsessed with making money. Maha was devoted to her little daughter.

"What little do we know about our future," Maha thought when she saw him again one day. "Maybe it is just as well, ignorance reduces fear and anxiety. In truth, no one knows who they really are or the real meaning and purpose of their experiences."

64
Arjun's Burden

Arjun carried a heavy burden within him, a burden so profound that it shadowed even the brightest moments of his life. Each day felt like a struggle, each breath a battle against the darkness that threatened to consume him. Unable to bear the weight of his despair any longer, Arjun sought the guidance of the village guru.

In the humble abode of the Guru, Arjun poured out his heart, expressing his desperate desire to escape the pain of existence, to disappear from this world altogether. The Guru listened patiently, gently nodding his head. With a soft yet firm voice he said, "Arjun, this is an arena in which you are not equipped to enter. Let's look at it from another perspective of what life actually is. You are a by-product of life, and questioning the authority of having or not having life, is not allowed."

As Arjun listened intently, the Guru explained that life is a divine manifestation, a radiant expression of the entity most prevalent and yet most unknown - God. "Suicide is inconsequential," the Guru continued, "because life cannot be severed, it is timeless and eternal and will continue."

With each word, the Guru unravelled the tangled knots of Arjun's despair, showing him that suicide, in any form, is but a fleeting blip of darkness in the eternal effulgence of life. "Life manifests in infinite strands," the Guru mused, "and death, including suicide, is simply one strand on the dark side of life. Suicide is the opposite of grace and goodness. Your thoughts about taking your own life are a way of objecting, because you have misidentified yourself with your shadow-self. But you have forgotten about your eternal perfect soul. If you truly are graced to be touched by the present moment, then the highest level of intelligence has transformed you to timelessness. You have to accept that the essence of you, your soul or spirit, is timeless, boundless and eternally alive."

As the realization dawned upon him, Arjun felt a weight lift from his shoulders. In the presence of the Guru, he glimpsed the truth of his own existence - that beyond the transient struggles of the ego-self, there lay a boundless and timeless essence, a divine presence within him.

With gratitude in his heart, Arjun cried with relief, his spirit uplifted by the wisdom he had received. For in that moment, he understood that the ultimate grace was to be touched by the present, to transcend the confines of time and duality, and to merge with the cosmic ocean of unity that is both timeless and boundless.

65

The Saint of Bombay

I met the authentic Indian mendicant in Bombay, or Mumbai as it is now known, at the iconic four hundred year old shrine, Haji Ali Dargah, which "floats" in the sea and where the Sufi saint Haji Ali Shah Bukhari is buried. It is actually built on an islet about one kilometre off the coast and can be reached by foot during low tide via a narrow causeway. The shrine had become a popular pilgrimage spot for dedicated believers of all faiths. It is said that if you go with the right intention and sincerity you will find proof of the saint's soul still living there.

For many years I had intended to visit Haji Ali, but I was put off by the long walk on a narrow stony causeway lined with beggars and lepers on both sides. Eventually the opportunity presented itself. I had been invited to dinner at someone's house close to the shrine, and made plans to visit the shrine beforehand. I wanted to walk to the shrine, and for that one had to carry enough coins to put into the hands of the outstretched arms. Therefore a few bags of coins had to be procured first.

The amount of people begging was heart-breaking, and I wasn't even halfway to the shrine when all the money was finished. I wanted to give something to each and every one of them, so I had to exchange some more notes for coins before I could continue. When I reached the shrine the second batch of money was also gone.

Inside the shrine I felt the light and presence of the saint. When people of that calibre leave their body, it is like an atom bomb that had detonated – something always radiates there.

As I left the shrine, I noticed a human figure perched on a wall a few meters away, looking out at the waves. He looked dishevelled, but also somehow graceful. He was there, but in an absent way. I wanted to give him something too, and took a large note from my pocket. I went up to the wall, greeted him and proffered the money. He looked at it with a faint smile, and then looked at me with a quizzical expression, as if he did not understand why I had given it to him. He held the note between thumb and index finger, lifted it up and just let it go, fluttering away into the sea.

Then he came down from the wall, opened his arms wide, stepped right up to me and wrapped me in his cloak. In that moment it felt as if time had stopped and everything had vanished, except for a beam of awareness.

Within his cloak I was shifted to a level of consciousness that was not bounded by space or time.

www.ingramcontent.com/pod-product-compliance
Lightning Source LLC
Chambersburg PA
CBHW020150090426
42734CB00008B/766